WATER GARDENS

Frontispiece: The fiery tints of Swamp Cypress (*Taxodium distichum*) in autumn.

Roddy Llewellyn
WATER GARDENS

The Connoisseur's Choice

Photographs by Bob Challinor

WARD LOCK LIMITED · LONDON

First published in Great Britain in 1987
by Ward Lock Limited, 8 Clifford Street
London W1X 1RB, an Egmont Company

House editor Denis Ingram
Designed by Melissa Orrom
Text set in Goudy Old Style
by MS Filmsetting Limited, Frome, Somerset

Printed and bound in Spain

British Library Cataloguing in Publication Data

Llewellyn, Roddy
  Water gardens.
  1. Water gardens
  I. Title
  635.9'674   SB423

  ISBN 0-7063-6523-2

For Alexandra

Looking through a jagged 'window' in the grotto at Stourhead.

CONTENTS

Author's Acknowledgements

I want to give special thanks to Jeff Wakeham of Wakeham-Gilbert Ltd, Allan Sawyer of the Royal Horticultural Society, landscape architect Pamela Bullmore, Libby Hall, Anthony Archer-Wills, Mark and Jane Burns, Lavinia Wellicombe, Clifford Lee, Mr Takashi Sawono, director of the Japanese Garden Centre Ltd, Carom Water Crafts, landscape architect Robin Williams, Richard Ellis of Ellis Associates (architects), Jenny Hunt (Photographic Manager of the National Trust), Sue Bond, Richard Vessey (Administrator, Sutton Place), Sir Geoffrey Jellicoe, Clarence Macdonald (architect), and John Broome (Chairman, Alton Towers Ltd).

My many thanks to all those garden owners who between them must have brewed hundreds of gallons of tea. These include Christopher and Angharad Cazanove, Mrs Daffy Moore, Myles Challis, Jean Clark, Beth Chatto, the Hon. Aylmer Tryon, Lord Aberconway, Mike Abrams, Mrs Peter Clifford and the Hon. Mrs Legge-Bourke.

I would also like to thank Mr R.A. Pullin (Director, Hever Castle), Ray Davies and Peter Robinson of Stapeley Water Gardens, Paul Nicholls (Head Gardener, Hidcote Manor), David Hardman (Marketing Manager, Tatton Park), Sandra George (Public Relations Officer, Bicton Park), Mrs Watson (Warden, Scott's Grotto), Alan Sargent, David Norris, Barry Hicks (British Tourist Authority), Mr Anil Ishani (President, Ismaili Centre), Geoff Ace (Head of Landscape Construction, Merrist Wood Agricultural College), Aunt Vicky, Rosie Forbes and Rosie Atkins, and Pat O'Shaughnessey.

Some of the introductions to Chapter 1 and to Chapter 5 I have discovered from reading Anthony Huxley's *An Illustrated History of Gardening*, Paddington Press Ltd, 1978, which I can thoroughly recommend to readers.

Finally, thank you, Annabelle (Sutcliffe) who must have typed at least 300 letters and without whom I could not have coped with the research.

R.Ll.

Publisher's Acknowledgements

All the colour photographs were taken by Bob Challinor and the line drawings were drawn by Nils Solberg.

The publishers are very grateful to the owners of private gardens, cited above, who kindly granted permission for their gardens to be photographed and to the National Trust for granting permission for photographs to be taken at Hidcote, Sheffield Park, Stourhead and Tatton Park. We are also grateful to the Royal Horticultural Society for granting permission for photographs to be taken at their Wisley garden and at the Chelsea Flower Show.

PREFACE

My research for this book revealed all sorts of different water features, one of the most extraordinary being the Willow Tree Fountain at Chatsworth House in Derbyshire. I had never seen a replica of a willow in copper before, or of any other tree, for that matter, least of all one which spouts water from its branches.

The organization for the photography was the most difficult part. It was a question of writing to the various garden-owners in February asking them if one could photograph their gardens on a certain date, and then spending the next few months praying that the sun would shine at 10 am on Thursday, 24 July in Staffordshire. The Almighty did not always comply with our wishes, and there were quite a few days spent sitting, waiting for the rain to stop. It has to be said that He was pretty good to us during the four months of photography. Even on the gloomiest days, Bob Challinor, my photographer, performed miracles with all the goodies he produced from his magic silver box which travelled with us the 10 000 miles or so around the UK. He never gave me a second's doubt that he could not make the best of any given situation. The photographs are proof of his expertise.

The use of water in a decorative form in the garden was not heard of in England until the early eighteenth century. As in so many other cases in recorded history where kings and emperors were perpetually trying to outdo each other, they behaved rather like children in the nursery wanting bigger and bigger toys. In this particular case, it was Charles II who, having heard about Louis XIV's landscape architect, André le Nôtre, invited him over to landscape St James's Palace.

Here le Nôtre laid out a formal water garden in the shape of a straight, ornamental canal running the length of the park, flanked by straight avenues of trees. This was later replaced by the informal ponds and bird sanctuary that we know today. There does exist a surviving example of his work at Bicton Park, near Exeter in Devon, which was not laid out until 1735, 35 years after his death. (It is now one of the very few Grade II listed gardens in the UK.)

By far one of the most charming water gardens I came across was at Frampton Court in Gloucestershire, the family home of the Clifford family since the Norman Conquest (1066). There I found, and wait for it, a Strawberry Hill Gothic Orangery – a mouthwatering combination – built in 1760 along with a formal canal stretching out in front of it. I found a different idea on the same theme at Bodnant, in North Wales where in 1939 the second Lord Aberconway reconstructed a Pin Mill (which he had found in a dilapidated condition in Gloucestershire) at the end of his canal.

It was about the turn of this century that the Japanese style of gardening came to our shores. It was introduced, in many cases, by members of the upper classes who returned with a retinue of Japanese gardeners and servants as well as disassembled tea houses, bridges and other ornaments, having completed their stint with the Foreign Service. While the gardeners were laying out the gardens and erecting the buildings, the servants were presumably producing endless cups of tea to keep everyone happy.

The very idea of having all that hand luggage these days would, sadly, be out of the question. Of all the styles of water gardens that I have discovered during my research, I found the Japanese to be the most relaxing and pleasing. This, of course, is exactly the atmosphere the Zen Buddhist priests wanted to achieve. The joy of their layouts is that they are so simple: a few specially chosen and positioned plants, stones, bridges and buildings, interspersed with the occasional ornament. Each ornament has some sort of symbolism attached to it. Westerners don't necessarily understand exactly what each one means, but this does not change our enjoyment of them in the slightest.

There is a marvellous example of a Japanese water garden at Compton Acres, near Bournemouth in Dorset. You enter part of it through a Toro Gate. Wrapped around pillars on either side is an unwelcoming-looking dragon. These represent bad or evil, whereas the two doves perched on the top of the arch, represent good. The zig-zag stepping stones (otherwise known as a Flying Goose Bridge) which span the pond, are not connected to the shore either side to keep away evil spirits. At Compton Acres there is a frog sitting in the water close to the Flying Goose Bridge, laughing at the stranded evil spirits.

While writing this book I found that the longer-established gardens were more rewarding and it was no coincidence that they had been built by gentlemen of taste and money, a bygone era. I did not manage to find any modern water gardens on a large scale that appealed to me. The ones I did find were charmless and had a municipal flavour, very often with sharp and jagged lines. All the water garden owners that I talked to had one thing in common. They all agreed that they could never have a garden without water in it. Once you have had a washing-up machine or a sunshine roof on your car, you find that life isn't quite the same without them. The same applies to water in a garden.

I have described a wide variety of smaller, domestic water gardens. All sorts of them popped up in the most unlikely places during the course of my research. In the southern outskirts of London I discovered a piece of Westmorland scenery splashing its way down amongst the bijoux residences. It took the owner five years to build, on and off, and a lot of care and love had gone into its construction. The end result was extremely effective. In Barkway, Essex, I discovered a tiny garden laid out in the Japanese style. It was an ingeniously built garden, measuring 3 × 6 m (10 × 20 ft). Its water feature consisted of a submersible pump sitting in a plastic bucket. The bucket was below ground level and disguised with gravel and stones, so that all one sees is the playing water. This was the smallest water feature I came across!

One of the other joys of writing this book was the discovery of a few grottoes. Grotto-building was at its most rampant during the mid-eighteenth century but sadly, few remain unvandalized today. In most cases, they were left as respected objects of beauty until only a few decades ago when that particular generation decided that it was going to deface everything of beauty around them. I wonder why that was? However, I did find two magnificent grottoes, one of them at the edge of a lake. It contained little gurgling springs and crowning its main chamber were magnificent stalactites stabbing their way down from the ceiling. Both the walls and stalactites were smothered in fingers of felspar and in one or two of the chambers outcrops of semi-precious stones were found.

Lakes proved to be a difficult subject as, basically, they are all the same, or rather so I thought at the beginning of my research. One of the lakes I chose was the one at Sheffield Park in Sussex, about which Lancelot ('Capability') Brown had the first word in around 1775. Since then various owners of the property have taken a lot of care to restore and to add, so now it is our generation who can fully benefit from the fruits of their labours. It is a great shame that so few people today think about planting for posterity in the same way. It was succeeding generations of the Hoare family who took similar interest in the lake at Stourhead in Wiltshire. Both were created by damming rivers in a wonderful era when people had space to play around with, and also a vast, cheap labour force at their disposal.

From a practical point of view, liners for containing water come in all sorts of different shapes and sizes. We have already discussed the plastic bucket. In the old days they used to line the hole with clay and then proceeded to 'puddle' it in. This involved an army of men wearing stout boots firming straw into the clay with the heel of their boots. Sometimes, lime was spread first to decrease the amount of worm activity. Modern-built lakes (and reservoirs) are often lined with a flexible liner, the strongest, best and most expensive to date being Butyl. A single strip is ideal for lining a false stream (see p.56). It is also used for lining reservoirs in drier climates. In this country it lasts about 80 years, and about the only thing which destroys or weakens it is oil. The ready-made, fibreglass pond is as popular as ever, but I am very glad to be able to report that the dreaded kidney-shaped variety is waning in popularity. Manufacturers, presumably sensing a more sophisticated market, now make them in rounds and other shapes. I have a round one in my garden in London (see p.46). It measures 60 cm (2 ft) deep, and 1·2 m (4 ft) in diameter. It sits in the centre of a circle paved in radiating brick. This circle's diameter is the same as the width of the garden. From a landscape point of view, this helps to 'push' the boundaries of the garden outwards making it seem much larger than it really is. The pond contains large stones at the bottom and has a top fill of rounded seaside pebbles, with a skin of chicken-wire mesh separating the two. Marginal plants sit amongst the pebbles and a single thin jet of water allows a ping pong ball to sit and play on it. My reason for infilling the pond is that my children are very young; it now means that they can be left alone without constant supervision.

Concrete-lined pools (see p.131) must be built correctly if they are to last. Even then, harsh winters can cause cracks within their casing and the resulting leakages are not always easily cured.

In conclusion, it cannot be denied that water brings life to a garden in the same way that a record player brings life inside the house. Both supply different kinds of music, and both succeed in creating a more relaxed atmosphere.

The difficulty when it comes to 'freezing' a photograph of water on celluloid is that you may lose its two most valuable properties: movement and noise. However, I think these photographs speak for themselves.

R. Ll.

A section of the meandering stream at Bodnant, luring the visitor onwards.

1

HISTORICAL WATER GARDENS

Ever since the world began it has been a terrific advantage to have a water supply near to hand, for obvious reasons. As the world started to become a more civilized place to live in, the basic architecture of houses and the layout of gardens changed accordingly. It was not until the seventeenth century that formal stretches of water appeared in England, largely as a result of le Nôtre's influence, although, fountains had certainly been built before then.

The development of gardens owes much to ancient symbolism, which becomes more evident as one moves East. The designs of many ancient gardens were based on the cosmic cross, whose first literary appearance is in the second chapter of Genesis: 'And a river went out of Eden to water the garden; and from thence it was parted and became into four heads'. This theme of a garden being divided into four parts by water is recurring. The Persians still make carpets depicting such gardens with a river or canal forming a cross.

During the Han Dynasty in the second century BC in China, it is recorded that many gardens there contained water along with strategically laid rocks, pavilions and bridges. Sadly, records are poor, largely as a result of an ancient custom which dictated that a son cannot continue living in a property in which his father died. The records we do have suggest that the style then tended towards the romantic landscape with grottoes, waterfalls, and bamboo, the one most consistent feature being one large rock which represented a mountain.

Thousands of miles away in South America the Incas were growing vegetables and fruit on a large scale, as early as 2500 BC. Their gardens often contained water channels and artificial plants made of solid gold and silver.

The Aztecs created one of the most extraordinary aspects of gardening with the help of water, after having been stripped of their lands and wealth by the invading Spanish. They were forced to live on the marshy lake shores and, in order to create additional areas for growing crops, they innovated floating rafts made of a framework of roots and covered in reeds and then soil. Thus, they became extensions of the land. Many were mobile and were used as floating vegetable gardens which were transported on water from home to market and back. The floating gardens of Xochimilco can still be seen today on the outskirts of Mexico City.

In ancient Rome, urbanization on a grand scale resulted in apartment blocks with window boxes. They also had a wide range of containers which often included fish ponds. The earliest examples of water gardens still in existence today are in Mogul India, the most famous being that of the Taj Mahal. When the Moguls reached Kashmir, they exploited the hillsides that descended to the waters of Lake Dal. Here were built magnificent waterfalls, and the flat surfaces were chiselled out of the rock in such a way as to form patterns in the flowing water. I have seen modern examples of this in the USA, usually with water flowing over brick. The Moguls also used to design their water chutes so that behind the falling curtain of water and set into niches, onlookers could gaze at candles by night and artificial flowers made of precious metals by day.

Many early water gardens in Italy are extremely elaborate and geared around a practical joke which involved concealed jets, controllable from a distance, which made life rather damp for the unsuspecting visitor. These jets were sometimes hidden under seats – one famous example being the table of a nobleman where each chair, except his, had a small hole in it. The water was turned on and posteriors became damp but, as it was the protocol in those days that no one lower in social precedence could rise to their feet unless he did, there was nothing they could do. Water suddenly sprang up ladies' crinolines from paving, grottoes became showers, artificial trees suddenly started to drip, and statues sprayed innocent visitors from their nipples without warning.

The most famous landscape architect associated with large expanses of water was the eighteenth-century Lancelot or 'Capability' Brown. The story goes that he was so-called as he was often supposed to have said to clients, 'It has great capabilities,' when looking around their estates. Those who look upon him as a vandal have a point, but much of his work exists today in its maturity, whereas the parterres and formal gardens which he got rid of would probably be impossible to keep up today.

The son of a farmer, he started his career at Stowe (now a public school), where he was greatly influenced by William Kent who had recently returned from Italy with all sorts of new and exciting ideas. It was he who introduced Brown to 'natural landscape'. He dammed rivers and streams (or sometimes changed their courses), built artificial hills, and dotted clumps of trees here and there – always with a huge labour force at his disposal. By 1783, when he died, he had re-designed most of the famous gardens in England.

SHEFFIELD PARK, NEAR HAYWARDS HEATH, SUSSEX

This splendid garden was originally laid out by Lancelot ('Capability') Brown in about 1775, for John Baker Holroyd (later created first Earl of Sheffield). James Wyatt designed the neo-Gothic house at the same time. Brown built the two lakes furthest from the house with an interconnecting rocky cascade, by damming a tributary of the Ouse. He also laid down large lawns that swept down to the water's edge, and planted carefully sited clumps of native oaks, beeches and pines.

The grandson of the first Earl employed Pelham & Sons of Chelsea to alter radically Brown's landscape by sweeping away the lawns near to the house during the late nineteenth century, and replacing them with a further two lakes. Between these two lakes was built a magnificent waterfall 7·5 m (25 ft) tall and constructed in Sussex sandstone and clay alone. At the same time he set about a massive planting programme, mostly around his two new lakes. This time trees of a more exotic

Sheffield Park: The closest thing to a cartoonist's desert island in the UK, complete with palm tree.

Sheffield Park: The mirroring properties of water used to their best advantage in autumn.

16

Sheffield Park: An inviting view planned by Lancelot 'Capability' Brown. I wish he could see it in its maturity.

nature were chosen in contrast to those planted by Brown. These included most of those which give a colourful autumn display, such as Japanese maples (*Acer palmatum* spp), swamp cypress (*Taxodium distichum*), and Brewer's spruce (*Picea breweriana*). The third, major planting programme occurred in about 1909 when Mr Arthur G. Soames bought the property. He added mainly spring- and summer-flowering trees and shrubs such as dog-woods, rhododendrons and kalmias. Today these rhododendrons have grown into magnificent domed groups, some of them tumbling down to the water's edge where their reflection doubles the glory of their springtime display.

So, here we have a story of succeeding gener-ations of caring gardeners, each injecting their own ideas and passions into the same garden. In those days, somehow, there was more planting done for posterity, with the result that we can all enjoy their work today.

Sheffield Park: A duck cuts a silver streak in the water in this tranquil misty morning scene.

CHATSWORTH HOUSE, DERBYSHIRE

The gardens at Chatsworth House, as we see them today, are mainly the creation of the sixth Duke of Devonshire (1790–1858). Today there are 21 gardeners who tend the 105 acres. The architect Sir Jeffry Wyatville and the famous gardener Sir Joseph Paxton, who were both in his employ, were responsible for the nitty-gritty of the construction.

However, the cascade, perhaps the most important of all the landscape features at Chatsworth, survives as part of the original garden as laid out by the first Duke in the late seventeenth century. It was designed for him by Grillet, a pupil of le Nôtre. It escaped the clutches of Lancelot ('Capability') Brown, the landscape architect famous as the

Chatsworth: Grillet's famous cascade consisting of 24 deep steps, each 7·2 m (24 ft) wide.

Chatsworth: The Emperor Fountain 88 m (290 ft) high, served by a lake 116 m (381 ft) higher than the fountain head.

reviver of natural style, who completed his assignment during the 1760s under the auspices of the fourth Duke.

There is no getting away from the fact that 'Capability' Brown caused the widespread destruction of countless walled, formal gardens and other formal features to make way for natural landscape. On the other side of the house, Brown had his own way, and created the great open expanse of parkland through which the River Derwent meanders. He altered the course of the river to get it just right.

The cascade consists of 24 deep steps, each

7·2 m (24 ft) wide. It is beautifully constructed so that the water flows perfectly evenly down each one. The water is gravity-fed from a pond on the top of the hill. The temple at the top of the cascade normally has water spashing down over its domed roof.

The other most eye-catching water feature at Chatsworth is the Emperor Fountain which sits in the Canal Pond built for the first Duke in 1703. The story behind its existence is that when the sixth Duke went to Russia with Paxton he greatly admired one of the fountains of Czar Nicholas. The Duke wanted to build a bigger and better one

Chatsworth: The copper Willow Tree Fountain can soak unsuspecting onlookers . . .

for the Czar's visit to England the following year in 1844. Although it was completed by the June of that year in time for the imperial visitor he never saw it because, by the time the Czar had got as far as York, he was too tired to continue his journey. Nonetheless, the fountain and the lake which feeds it were named after him. The construction of the lake at the top of the hill involved moving about 80 000 cu. m (100 000 cu. yd) of soil by shovel, wheelbarrow, and horse-cart, and the building of a masonry dam 495 m (550 yd) along the hillside. The drop between the lake and the fountain head is 116 m (381 ft), enabling the fountain to throw a jet to a height of 88 m (290 ft) as a simple result of water trying to find its own level. The pipe which connects the two has a 38 cm (15 in) bore, 61 m (200 ft) of it being at a gradient of one in two. The valves take five minutes to open or close to prevent any possible shock damage to the pipes. In turn, the lake is fed by a 5·6 km (3½ mile) open stone drain which runs through the wettest part of the moors. It is pretty well level so that the supply of water to the lake remains a constant, steady flow, even after heavy storms.

The waterfall which splashes down on the Wellington Rock is a cooling place to be on a hot day. If you look at the rock formation closely you can see that it is a natural outcrop which has been cut into blocks and reassembled.

Of all the water features here, I found the Willow Tree Fountain the most exciting. It is a replacement of the original which was made for the first Duke and was made locally, by Bower of Chesterfield, in the 1830s. The original was situated in Wise's great parterre of 1694, to the south of the house. It is, like every other water feature in this garden, fed by gravity from a pond above. All you have to do is turn a valve, hidden in bushes nearby, to soak the unsuspecting visitors below. It does have maintenance problems, especially during the winter when the copper branches are ruptured in much the same way as a burst pipe.

ALTON TOWERS, STAFFORDSHIRE

The gardens at Alton Towers were designed by Charles Talbot, fifteenth Earl of Shrewsbury and his nephew the sixteenth Earl, between 1814 and 1835. It is certain that landscape architects were employed to supervise the work, one of whom was almost certainly Robert Abrahams (1774–1850).

It proved to be one of the most extraordinary projects of its era and was considered by some to be in very bad taste. John Loudon, who visited Alton in 1833, described it thus: 'In excessively bad taste, or rather, perhaps, as the work of a morbid imagination joined to the command of unlimited resources.' He must have been describing the entire layout of the house and park which contained many other features, including a druidical stone circle in the style of Stonehenge, a Gothic Tower and several fountains, one aptly named the Corkscrew Fountain.

Now that the trees and shrubs have matured, it has become the fascinating, fairy-tale garden that it was first intended to be. Perhaps the most striking of all the features at Alton Towers, now an extremely successful Leisure Park, is the Chinese Pagoda Fountain. It is thought to have been built to Abraham's designs, who copied it from the To Ho Pagoda in Canton. Directly fed by a water supply on higher ground, it sends up a powerful 21 m- (70 ft-) high jet which soars above the tree tops. As the water falls, it can activate the bells below, depending on whether the water happens to hit them. The bridge which used to link the pagoda to the shore no longer exists.

(Opposite) Alton Towers: A feature of the fantasy landscape as laid out by the 15th & 16th Earls of Shrewsbury between 1814 and 1835.

SHRUBLAND HALL, NEAR IPSWICH, SUFFOLK

Many consider this to be the finest example of an Italianate garden in the UK. There is evidence on the site of pre-Roman, Roman and Saxon occupation, and an avenue of huge and very ancient sweet chestnut (*Castanea sativa*) is thought to have been planted by the monks from a now vanished monastery in about 1000 AD. From the fifteenth to the late eighteenth centuries, Shrubland was the home of the Bacon family (close relatives of Sir Francis Bacon). Only a fragment of the original Old Hall remains.

The property was bought by Sir William Middleton, Bart, whose family laid out the famous garden at Middleton Place, South Carolina, USA. It is still owned by a descendant, and open to the public.

Shrubland Hall: A backdrop of tall dark trees add drama to the view down the 100 steps but the central shining fountain is the point of focus that holds the whole elaborate design together.

A bridge on which one can sit in order to study intimately the aquatic inmates below.

In 1850 Sir William Fowle Middleton, Bart, employed the services of Sir Charles Barry to enlarge his house and create magnificent terraced garden modelled on the Villa d'Este in northern Italy.

Sir William is said to have maintained a staff of 60 gardeners whose numbers had shrunk to 20 before 1914. Today there are only 3 or 4. Through Sir William, Shrubland descended by marriage to the present owner, the sixth Lord de Saumarez, and the house is now run as a health clinic.

Since 1850 succeeding generations have all been keen gardeners. During the early 1930s the Rockery, which looks quite impressively alpine, with a bridge over a ravine and a Swiss-style cottage below, was reconstructed and replanted by Will Ingwerson senior, the Swiss alpine expert. From a long pool at the top, water splashes down over the rocks into a fern-shaded pool at the bottom. In 1888 some plantings and minor alterations were made by fourth Lord de Saumarez (my great-grandfather).

The West front of the house looks out onto two ballustraded terraces and an elaborate baroque portico from which descends a flight of 100 steps. These are 3·65 m (12 ft) wide, with four rests 6·1 m (20 ft) wide. The many flower-filled stone urns on either side give colour during the summer as you descend. At the bottom the shallow steps bear left and right like arms, embracing a large round, stone-rimmed pool. I well remember playing in this fountain as a child. A simple jet of water rises high from its centre.

A long vista of lawns stretch at right angles to the steps, and beyond the pool are formal beds, a loggia in the early Renaissance style, ballustrading and classical statues. A backdrop of tall dark trees adds drama to the view but the central shining fountain is the point of focus that holds the whole elaborate design together.

An eighteenth-century Strawberry Hill Gothic orangery at the end of an ornamental canal at Frampton Court.

Frampton Court, Frampton-on-Severn, Gloucestershire

This lovely Strawberry Hill Gothic Orangery stands in the grounds of Frampton Court at the far end of a Dutch water canal. It was built in 1760, some 30 years after the Court. Originally, it contained staging throughout the ground floor. Its architect is reputed to be William Halfpenny and the Dutch Water Garden is comparable in design to Westbury Water Garden which is the opposite side of the River Severn.

The walls are honeycombed with the flues for a small oven at the back of the building. The smoke passed out through an ornamental cupola at the top. There are two octagonal rooms on the first floor which were used for tea parties in olden days. The building has now been converted into a dwelling house which is let for holidays.

Frampton has been the family seat of the Clifford family since the Conquest. Indeed, it was Mrs Peter Clifford who showed me around the garden.

BLENHEIM PALACE, NEAR WOODSTOCK, OXFORDSHIRE

Blenheim Palace is perhaps most famous for being the birthplace of Britain's most illustrious recent prime minister, Sir Winston Churchill. His name-sake was the father of the first Duke of Marl-borough who was given for his services, Blenheim Palace and the surrounding estate by a grateful Queen (Anne) and nation. The house was to be called Blenheim after the Danube village where he had such a glorious victory over the French and Bavarians on 13 August 1704. Young John (later

Sir John) Vanbrugh was chosen as architect and not, surprisingly enough, Sir Christopher Wren. The Queen's choice of Vanbrugh might be ex-plained as he had quite recently produced some promising designs for Greenwich Hospital on the Thames and Castle Howard in Yorkshire, to mention just two.

From contemporary correspondence it is easy to see that Sarah, first Duchess of Marlborough, had a lot to do with the building of Blenheim. It is

(Above) Blenheim Palace: The very formal water parterre with 'Capability' Brown's lake in the background.
(Opposite) Blenheim Palace: The most breathtaking of all the landscaped lakes in England.

well-known that she and the Duke fell out of favour with Queen Anne which resulted in the money flow running dry, and in 1712 building at Blenheim ceased totally.

The Grand Bridge which spans the lake was built under the direction of Vanbrugh between 1708 and 1712 by the mason, Bartholomew Peisley. As we see it today it is complete apart from the arcaded superstructure, according to a contemporary elevation drawing. These final touches were vetoed by Sarah following her disagreement with Vanbrugh: 'I made Mr Vanbrugh my enemy by the constant disputes I had with him to prevent his extravagance.' Vanbrugh retorted, 'You have your end Madam for I will never trouble you more unless the Duke of Marlborough recovers [from a stroke] so far to shelter me from such an intolerable treatment.' When the building was resumed in 1716 the Duke had to pay for its completion himself.

The construction of the Grand Bridge still proves to be an enigma today. It contains many rooms the possible use of which is difficult to guess. It originally spanned a canal designed by Sarah, but there is evidence that Vanbrugh had planned a less formal lake. In 1764, Lancelot ('Capability') Brown characteristically built a dam at one end, so flooding the area with the help of the River Glyme, and creating one of the most beautifully landscaped areas in the whole of the UK. Poor Vanbrugh must have turned in his grave to see his beautiful bridge partially submerged! Elizabeth's Island in the lake was the only section of the two existing causeways that Brown chose to leave – the icing on the cake.

The water parterre was planned by the ninth Duke, with the assistance of the French landscape architect Achille Duchêne. It replaced a messy shrubbery.

This is a wonderful example of a formal water garden, which lends itself perfectly to its surroundings.

BOWOOD, CALNE, WILTSHIRE

Bowood has been the seat of the Fitzmaurice family since 1754. A large and splendid eighteenth century house stands dominant over its gardens. They are extensive, perhaps the most impressive part of them being the lake, which is approached by a vast stretch of lawn. A large expanse of green meets a large expanse of blue.

Upon seeing the lake and the reflected Doric temple on its opposite shore, one's nose begins to twitch, as if one has smelt a Brown. Those tell-tale techniques of his are all around. And, of course, one is right; our 'Capability' got his hands on an insipid little pond and proceeded to transform it into the lake we see now. Funnily enough the Doric temple, whose architect is not known, was moved here from another part of the estate and was not part of Brown's original plan. He has used his usual tricks and by damming this and damming that produced a magnificent stretch of water.

Brown often used to suggest a cascade to a client as an optional extra, rather like a car salesman suggesting a sunshine roof for a car today. But it was not Brown who built the cascade here. It was not until after he had departed from Bowood (no doubt to demolish some parterre-containing walled-in garden somewhere else) that The Hon. Charles Hamilton, a very capable amateur landscape architect and the creator of Painshill, was invited in to build it. The rock work was set up by Josiah Lane, a specialist from Tisbury.

(Opposite) Bowood: A cascade which belongs more to the moors than the man-made gardens of a stately home.

BICTON, NEAR EXETER, DEVON

This 'Italian' Garden was thought to have been designed by André le Nôtre who came to England in 1680.

Le Nôtre (1613–1700) was best known for his creation of the garden at the Palace of Versailles, for Louis XIV. He also laid out a formal water garden in front of St James's Palace but this has been replaced by the informal lake which survives today. Originally, it consisted of a straight orna-mental canal running the length of the park with trees planted in straight avenues.

Le Nôtre was the first garden architect to use water in a sculptured form in Britain.

The garden at Bicton was not actually laid out until 1735, 35 years after he died. The central fountain is fed by gravity from a nearby spring. The square pond is flanked by a canal on three sides.

Bicton Park: Thought to be the earliest known example in the UK of a formal water setting by André le Nôtre.

A stream, appearing to originate from an outcrop of heathers and conifers, feeds the pond below.

33

Stourhead: The stunning view from the Temple of Apollo. It is difficult to tear yourself away.

STOURHEAD, STOURTON, WILTSHIRE

Once this book has been put to bed, so to speak, I think I shall remember the lake and surrounding gardens at Stourhead more than any other, so breathtaking are they. They were created by Henry Hoare II (1705–1785) who built them during the 1740s. He was the son of Henry Hoare I who built the present house and his grandfather, Sir Richard Hoare, (1648–1718) was the founder of Hoare's Bank and the son of a successful horse dealer.

Henry Hoare II quite simply dammed the River Stour. This resulted in what we see today: one large lake with a few other smaller ones connected to it. He worked with the architect,

Henry Flitcroft and was also responsible for the planting of contrasting native trees such as oak, beech and various conifers. You could say that this treatment of the landscape was verging on the Brownesque. Indeed it is, and it occurred at least 10 years or so before our Lancelot started to make his name. Henry Hoare II was succeeded by his grandson, Sir Richard Colt Hoare, second Baronet, who was responsible for planting a variety of exotic trees as well as rhododendrons – mauve R. ponticum and red R. arboreum. Hugh Richard Hoare was the next member of the family to take any interest in the gardens. He lived here between

Stourhead: Neptune beckoning his hairdresser.

Stourhead: Scented azaleas keep the olfactory organs satisfied whilst the views delight the eye.

Stourhead: A view the eye never tires of.

1841 and 1857 and during that time he added mostly evergreens believing, quite rightly, that they helped so much in improving the landscape during the dreary winter months. It was the last member of the Hoare family to live at Stourhead, Henry Hugh Arthur Hoare, sixth Baronet, who replaced many of the existing rhododendrons, during the 1920s and 1930s, with Himalayan hybrids. We can be grateful to him, especially, for the colourful and scented panorama of today.

The walk around the lake is a feast for the eyes. Despite the fact that there are a lot of other people there (it is after all, one of the National Trust's most visited properties), everyone seems to be very pleased to see each other. It is as if they are members of the same *élite* club.

The path has been cleverly laid. From time to time you are led through thick planting with great walls of tree and shrub on either side. Then, suddenly, a gap appears and through it the eye is led straight across the lake to some magnificent temple far away on the opposite shore. One is kept constantly entertained in this way. At one stage the path dips into the grotto. Very soon all is cool and dark, you have trouble seeing where you are going, and ahead is a faint white statue of Neptune. Just before you get to him, on the left, is a rough stone, a round window and through it, framed in jagged rock, another ravishing vista.

A little further on is a scaled-down replica of the Parthenon in Rome as well as the great Temple of Apollo. The latter is approached by a path easily missed which begins by a sudden outcrop of rock. From up here there is possibly the best view of all. The classicists think that the mass of different colour of the rhododendrons detract from the original, much simpler, planting. I see their point, but I'll be rushing back there in late spring or early summer of next year, to see them reflected in the water in all their glory.

Hever Castle, near Edenbridge, Kent

The gardens at Hever Castle were created by William Waldorf Astor between 1903 and 1908. He also extended the castle and built a 100-room Tudor village behind it. He created formal and informal gardens, using water where possible.

Perhaps the most fantastic is the Italian Garden and the Pompeii Wall, in front of which he housed his statuary which he collected while American Ambassador (Minister as it was then called) to Italy between 1882 and 1885.

Hever Castle: Shade and damp-loving plants co-exist happily in the shade of moss-covered water-dripping rocks above.

There is also a 35-acre lake which took two years to hand-dig by 800 men. He changed the natural course of the River Eden in order to make room for all his ideas. There are waterfalls, pools, a Venetian loggia and a maze. Astor also initiated the digging of an outer moat to surround the already existing one. This could well be described as a wide range of garden experiences! The water which feeds the various water features throughout the garden often follows circuitous and complex routes. For example, the water which feeds the cascade is pumped from the outer moat through pipes under the Tudor village. It then turns back on itself, goes round the inner moat, and on towards the cascade.

The stone for the grottoes was quarried from the nearby Ide Hill near Sevenoaks. It consists of 20 arches which contain 18 half pools, each fed by two stone cherubs with water pumped from the lake. The overflow from each half pool drains into a duct and back into the lake. Each half pool is separated by a carved stone buttress. The grottoes were inspired by the Gallery of a Hundred Fountains at the Villa d'Este at Tivoli near Rome. The planting consists mainly of shade-loving plants including the large glaucous-blue leaved hosta (*H. sieboldiana* 'Glauca'), the yellow Welsh poppy (*Meconopsis cambrica*) and primulas including the variety 'Postford White'.

The 'Roman Bath' sunken garden, surrounded by yew hedging includes some of the fantastic statuary collected by William Waldorf Astor. There is much more throughout the garden – all of it is protected with special sheeting throughout the winter.

(*Opposite*) Hever Castle: A view through one of the twenty arches revealing a half-pond fed by two stone cherubs beyond.

BODNANT, TAL-Y-CAFN, GWYNEDD

I visited Bodnant on a sunny day in late spring. Despite the fact that everything was one month late because of the cruel preceding winter of 1985–1986, there was plenty to see. There exists a special ambience at Bodnant – I felt it the minute I arrived. This may account for the fact that there are seldom any vacancies for gardeners, and there are 18 of them as I write. But even more unique is the Puddle family who have been Head Gardeners for three successive generations. Frederick came here in 1920 and he was succeeded by his son Charles, who in turn was succeeded by his son Martin, who became Head Gardener in 1982. Martin has two sons who are still very young. I'm sure there must exist some dreadful jokes about Puddles and water gardens. I was too polite to enquire.

There are 80 acres of garden open to the public at Bodnant. The garden consists of two distinctive areas: the Terrace Gardens and lawns near to the house, and the Dell which is formed by a tributary of the River Conwy. There are some wonderful views from the house towards the Snowdon range. There are four terraces altogether, the first one being the croquet terrace next to the house. Following on is the lily terrace, then the rose terrace and lastly the canal terrace with the magnolia borders below.

The present owner of the garden is The National Trust, but its administration is controlled by Lord Aberconway, whose great-grandfather, a Mr Henry Pochin, acquired the property in 1874. He planted most of the conifers in the garden, especially those in the Dell. He also planted the magnificent laburnum arch which delights visitors in late spring and early summer. After his death, in 1895, the property passed on to his daughter who married the first Lord Aberconway. It was her son who, between 1905 and 1914, built the Terrace Gardens as we see them today. He died in 1953 having passed the property over to the National Trust in 1949.

It is in the lowest of the terraces that we see the Canal Terrace. It consists of a long and narrow stretch of water, with waterlilies at each end, surrounded by lawn. It makes a very imposing stretch of water but must really have come to life when the Pin Mill (so-called because it was once used for the manufacture of pins) was erected at one end of it in 1939, some 25 years after the terraces were completed. It was brought here by the second Lord Aberconway from Woodchester in Gloucestershire, where it had been left in a sad state of delapidated neglect for some time. His own estate carpenters and stonemasons restored it to its original condition. The end result is bordering on the tajmahalesque, and very effective it is too. It provides an excellent example of using the reflective powers of water. On a higher terrace there is another example of this where a formal pond reflects the house. Unfortunately, the architecture of the house does not echo the beauty of the garden. The view from the other end of the canal is also rewarding. Here is an open air stage with splendid background of clipped yew (*Taxus baccata*). The painted seat is a copy of one designed by William Kent.

To the left of the Pin Mill there is a magnificent large *Magnolia kobus borealis*, which is smothered in white flowers in spring.

If you can drag yourself away from this impressive setting you will be rewarded by a series of informal water gardens which, like all the other water features here in this garden, are fed by a fresh-water reservoir up on higher ground two miles away. The Big Rockery consists of a series of waterfalls and ponds, all carefully thought out despite their totally natural look. Every fall and flow has been painstakingly arranged so that the water is diverted into as many different directions as possible. There is a skunk cabbage (*Lysichitum americanum*) which, apart from looking splendid with its yellow, shining arum-like flowers, is actually serving a purpose. It is dividing the water flow at that particular level into two separate channels.

The air here is strongly scented by large groups of skimmia. It is a tranquil scene and you

Bodnant: The Pin Mill re-erected by estate workers in 1939, having been found in a dilapidated state in Gloucestershire.

have to drag your reluctant feet away along the stream towards a waterfall. A long and uniform sheet of water falls from a dam in the Mill Pond (the actual mill is further down the stream). On the bridge over the waterfall is a seat suspended over the water. This is the ideal place for a discreet conversation without any danger of being overheard.

2

DOMESTIC WATER GARDENS

However small your garden, there is always room for a water feature of some kind. The garden on p.96 proves this. All the water gardens in this section are average- to small-sized.

There is no doubt that a successfully laid out garden will keep its visitors' eyes constantly busy. Water, especially if it is on the move, never fails to draw attention to itself. Although there are several methods of making a small garden look larger than it really is (I suggest you buy a copy of my last book *Beautiful Backyards* for further inspiration) there is nothing like water to add an extra point of interest to any garden.

The ideal space-saving water feature is the half pond up against a wall or fence fed by a stone mask or gargoyle (see p.116). Some manufacturers of these half ponds offer a tailor-made liner for them. They are rigid, made of fibre-glass and often shaped with a shelf to accommodate a selection of waterloving plants. If you want to scale this idea down even further, a clam shell (either the real thing or in stone) or similar-shaped receptacle will do a good job where space is very limited.

These water features are normally driven with the help of a submersible pump. They are electrically operated, and for convenience's sake the switch is positioned in the house next to the door which leads into the garden. Submersible pumps are often misunderstood. Quite simply, they recycle the same water to the fountain head and back. They are, therefore, ideal solutions for the vast majority of gardens which do not contain natural supplies of water particularly since it is seldom practical to operate a fountain or waterfall from the mains supply (see p.132).

I hope the following will interest you.

THE AUTHOR'S PRESENT GARDEN IN LONDON

This garden looked like any other in the row when I moved in just over one year ago. There was the usual central lawn with the gruesome, mean, little borders all around the edge – an-all-too-often-seen, unimaginative layout.

The garden gently sloped, and this gave me the idea of splitting it up into three separate terraces. Each is screened off with a trellis barrier, 1·8 m (6 ft) tall, up which climbers are trained. Very soon, each section will not be visible from the other with the result that the whole garden is not instantly visible at first glance. This 'screening off' method adds more interest to the garden and succeeds in making it appear to be larger than it really is.

The first part of the garden, the one you see in the photograph, is the formal terrace for entertaining. The second part is now thoroughly dug; it is used for vegetable production and has a picking border. The central path leads you up onto the

An elf keeping guard over the same children-safe pond, mulched with pebbles.

(Above) The brick-paved circle with central pebble fountain is a perfect place for children to play in complete safety.

seaside pebbles. These add a neat finish as well as acting as a camouflage for the water-loving plants' containers (see Fig. 1).

The fountain is propelled by a submersible pump which sits amongst the large stones at the bottom of the pool. The reason for the semi-circles of chicken-wire is that the pump can be removed without too much trouble for cleaning every autumn. Its electricity supply was installed at the very beginning of the garden's construction so as not to spoil the brick paving. It can be turned on by means of a switch indoors by the kitchen window. It is attached to a circuit breaker – you cannot take risks when there are children about.

The planting around the circle is always kept colourful during the summer. At each corner there is an evergreen – you can see a loquat (*Eriobotrya japonica*) on the right and the hardiest of all the 'gums', *Eucalyptus gunnii*, on the left. In the other two corners are a mimosa (*Acacia dealbata*) and an evergreen magnolia (*M. grandiflora* 'Exmouth').

third terrace which is the children's playing area. The path leads you directly to the wendy house which acts as a focal point to the whole garden; its small size suggests that it is further away than it is in reality. On either side of the wendy house are playing areas (suitable for a sandpit and other toys) mulched with pea shingle.

Going back to the first terrace, you will see the 1·2 m (4 ft) diameter round pond sitting in the middle of a 5·1 m (17 ft) diameter circle paved with Butterley 'Muirfield' brick pavers which were laid on 15 cm (6 in) of sand. The two bands of yellow represent ripples. The diameter of the circle is exactly the same size as the garden's width which has the effect of 'pushing' the garden's dimensions out sideways.

The circular pond is made of fibreglass; it is 60 cm (2 ft) deep with gently sloping sides. In its base are large stones over which two semi-circles of chicken wire were laid, 15 cm (6 in) from the rim of the pond. The top 15 cm (6 in) was infilled with

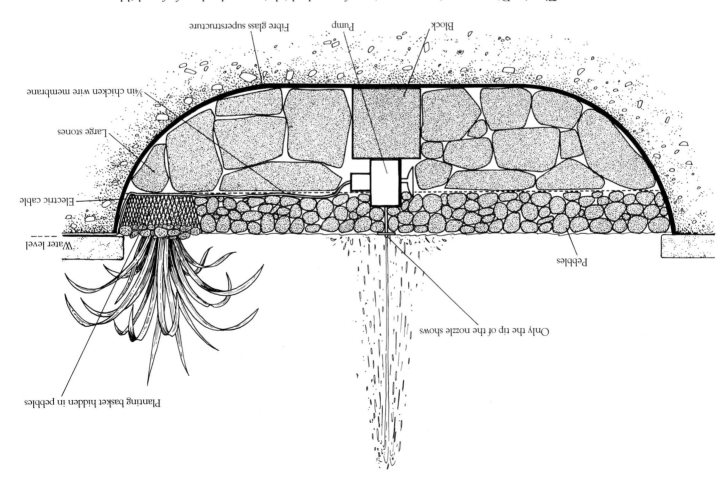

Fig. 1   Diagrammatic cross-section of a pool which is completely safe for children.

Fibre glass superstructure

Pump

Block

¼in chicken wire membrane

Large stones

Electric cable

Water level

Pebbles

Only the tip of the nozzle shows

Planting basket hidden in pebbles

D. A. Heath Esq of Kew, Surrey

Only two years ago this garden consisted of concrete paving and a hint of grass. It lies on the southern side of a modern house and measures 7 sq m (8 sq yd). The rounded wall was its only distinctive feature.

The reason the pond was raised was because of the school playground foundations underneath. The eventual shape of the pond was determined by the curvature of the garden wall. A circular pond would have taken up too much space, so the two halves were overlapped on an axis formed by a diagonal of the garden. A water tank was placed above the pond against the curve of the wall. This collects water from the old iron pump which then trickles over into the pond below.

The pond walls were built of solid 200 mm (8 in) concrete blocks, with brick facing in places where it might show. The wall facing the house was thickened to take a flat brick coping 400 mm (16 in) wide. The base of the pond is 75 mm (3 in) of lightly

This unusually shaped raised brick pond fits in neatly with this odd-shaped garden.

47

reinforced concrete, laid on the old playground surface. The sides of the pond were given two coats of a waterproof rendering followed by a further coat of waterproofer to prevent any possibility of leakage. Planting areas for marginals were built slightly below the expected water level.

The waterfall pump feature is served by a small submersible pump. A topping-up pipe was also connected to the mains. When the old pump was mounted against the wall, both supplies were connected to it. The marginal plants include houttuynia, iris, primula and ferns. Watercress and mimulus grow in the raised tank.

The design and much of the labour was done by the owner who employed a specialist landscape contractor as well as a bricklayer. The overall cost of the labour and materials including plant hire was in the region of £2000 (1984 prices).

Mr and Mrs M. Wright of Street, Gloucestershire

Until three years ago an old barn stood on this site. As soon as it had been demolished a 1·2 m (4 ft) bank was revealed. This natural lie of the land gave rise to the shapes and layout of the garden as we see it today. It was the slope, in particular, that inspired the owners of this garden to incorporate a waterfall of some kind. The construction of the garden 'evolved as it went', but the main aim was to create some sort of visual treat from the house.

The stone is Forest of Dean which the Wrights hand-selected themselves. By this method, 5 tons cost them £3! The shingle which sits on the bottom of the small ponds between the waterfalls was picked up one day from the beach after a picnic. The pond is lined with Butyl. It goes as deep as 75 cm (2½ ft) in the middle, to allow somewhere for the fish to escape to during harsh winters.

The pond has slowly silted up, enabling the plants growing in it to spread out their roots further. As a result, the bulrush has to be cut back quite severely during the summer.

The height from the bottom of the pond to the outlet at the top is 4·5 m (15 ft). Therefore, a powerful ¾-horsepower sump pump was chosen.

An existing bank inspired the waterfalls and the pond below.
(Opposite) A modern water garden which entertains all year round.

RALPH DIXON ESQ OF HATFIELD, DONCASTER

I liked this back garden in Yorkshire for several reasons, one of the main ones being that its owner had used very basic materials to their best effect. The two ponds are, in fact, fibreglass hedeourama, beautifully disguised to make them look like natural ponds.

Mr Dixon, a retired schoolmaster from Doncaster, wanted the water to look as if it 'had come from somewhere and was going somewhere'. This he achieved by positioning a false blink bridge next to the second pond. The path between the ponds gives the effect that they are connected; in reality they are not.

The garden is built next to a modern house, and designed to require as little maintenance as possible. Mr Dixon believes that English gardens should reflect their countryside. He believes, therefore, that the majority of them should consist of grass, some trees and bushes, and colour from just a few flowers.

A path between two separate ponds gives the illusion that the water is 'going somewhere'.

An unexpected piece of Westmorland countryside in the suburbs of London ...

RAYMOND FELDMAR ESQ OF SOUTH CROYDON, SURREY

It is difficult to believe that this garden sits in front of a modern house in the outer suburbs of London. It was built to look like a piece of Westmorland hillside where the water has eroded away the top soil to expose the rock below.

It was constructed by the owner of the house and it took him five years to finish, having worked on it only when he had the time. He often used to slide the rocks, many of which weighed up to 200 kg (4 cwt) each, on planks made slippery with mud. Crow-bars were used to achieve the right angles. Slivers of lead were used to get rocks positioned in exactly the right place, and if the owner could not find a rock of exactly the right size, he infilled with cement. The rock was bought for this garden in 1964, when a load of Westmorland rock cost only £55.

The water is circulated by a one-horsepower, air-cooled Stuart Turner pump. It is connected to a time switch so that the cascades start at 7·30 am and stop at 9 pm. The head of the fountain is 2·4 m (8 ft) high but there are several other runs which enable extra cascades to join the main stream.

The larger Japanese maples (acers) were planted 18 years ago and the planting between the rocks consists mainly of summer bedding plants.

THE HON. MRS LEGGE-BOURKE OF CRICKHOWELL, POWYS

This rock and water garden was designed one sunny afternoon by Wilfred Russell Bailey (third Baron Glanusk) who lived between 1891 and 1948, and built in 1932. Today it is owned and tended by his daughter and family.

There are three ponds here, each linked by a small concrete channel which meanders, like the River Usk in the park below, through lawn surrounded by dramatic rock formations on each side. The fall from the first pond to the third is a mere 6 cm (2½ in), the bottom pond having first been built as a swimming pool.

The concrete channels stand out as objects of beauty rather than utilitarian necessity, as they really do take on the appearance of a river winding through a lush and verdant valley. I used to play here as a child and was amused to see my own children doing exactly what I used to do at their

A small concrete channel leading to a pond, with a view of the Black Mountains beyond.

age: playing 'boat races' in these channels with flowers plucked from the rockery.

The stone was quarried from the hill opposite the house, and brought to the site by horse and cart. Before the landscaping was undertaken the site was just rough parkland. This is an idyllic setting, framed as it is with the Brecon Beacons in the background.

No pumps are used here. The water which feeds the first waterfall is supplied by the overflow of the private water supply which comes straight from the surrounding hills. (In fact there is no mains supply to any part of the estate.) Because of the purity of the water, trout were introduced into the first two pools but were soon eaten by heron. During very dry summers, the supply of water is somewhat weakened but luckily this does not happen very often in Wales!

The majority of the original planting on the rockery has died back over the years but it is being renewed bit by bit. 'There is still a lot to do,' the owner tells me.

Tulips and yellow allysum adorn this perfect setting with the Sugar Loaf mountain beyond.

The Hon Aylmer Tryon of Kingfisher's Mill, near Salisbury, Wiltshire

Kingfisher's Mill dates back to the early eighteenth century, though there was a mention of a mill on that site in the Domesday Book.

The Hon. Aylmer Tryon remembers Kingfisher's Mill as fully operational when he used to come here as a boy to play. He came back here to live over 30 years ago but had almost to completely rebuild the mill to make it habitable. There was no garden at all and the mill was merely surrounded by unkempt water meadow.

In those days, he knew precious little of gardening and had countless failures with plants as they were wrong for the soil (which is alkaline). He soon learnt that *Iris kaempferi* will not do on alkaline soils whereas *I. sibirica* and *I. laevigata* will.

The first year he planted crocuses but all the corms were soon eaten by mice. A friend suggested that he should place a holly leaf over each corm, but this had no effect. What did work was a gentle sprinkle of Jeyes' Fluid which resulted in the mice being unable to smell the bulbs.

Slowly, but surely, he learnt by trial and error, although he always had great success with all the willows which did not exist when he first came here. His technique of planting them is just to ram sticks of it into the ground every spring near to the water's edge. It never fails.

In those early days he asked a good friend of his, George Taylor, the director of Kew at the time, for advice. 'Do absolutely nothing; it's much too beautiful as it is,' was his reply. He did not totally heed his advice and rebuilt the waterways as they are today. He has kept the planting very informal, in keeping with the simple rustic setting. I found it a great relief to find Kingfisher's Mill so sympathetically treated; it makes visitors feel relaxed the minute they arrive. There are signs of the wild mixed with the artificial – *Rosa filipes* 'Kiftsgate' is allowed to scramble freely amongst the willow branches, and the magnolias M. *denudata* and M. 'Leonard Messell' add splashes of colour during the spring.

The garden is designed with wild life very much in mind – note the kingfisher perch jutting out over the water. (Around the other side of the house are beehives as well as plants especially grown for butterflies.) Many different species of bird come here and they are studied through binoculars from the picture window.

All the daffodils were given to Mr Tryon by the widow of the 'king of the daffodil growers', the late Lionel Richardson. Other parts of the garden have been planted up with primulas, water iris, kingcups, and other water-loving plants.

(Opposite) A swollen stream meanders through this simple and natural spring setting.

Who would guess that this spring and stream setting is just two years old?

G. HARMSWORTH ESQ OF PATCHING, WEST SUSSEX

This water garden was built three years ago. The combined materials and labour cost £6000.

The stream is lined with one length of Butyl measuring 18·3 m (60 ft) by 1 m (3 ft 4 in). It is guaranteed for 50 years and is quite capable of lasting well over 80 years, which is much longer than concrete. You will see that its edges have been well camouflaged by rocks around the water's edge. Butyl is readily available from major water

equipment stockists. It is black in colour and is very useful, therefore, for lining shallow water features, because the light is mirrored which gives the impression that the water is deeper than it really is.

There are concealed lights all the way down the 'stream' below water level.

The top fountain is only a few metres away from the house, to give you your bearings.

Mr and Mrs Christopher Cazanove of Wandsworth, London

One year ago this garden was a dark and gloomy area shaded by wild cherry and sycamore. It hardly ever saw the light of day. At the end of the garden, a garage with a classical façade overlooking the garden was built. It has two semi-circular arched windows either side of a similar-arched door, and a pediment with a central, false, circular window.

Despite this, and other new additions, there is no doubt that the garden owes most of its effect to the two water features. The round pond is 60 cm (2 ft) deep and 2·3 m (7 ft 10 in) in diameter. It was positioned off-centre on purpose in order to avoid too much symmetry. Its surrounding bands of brick adjoin the lower terrace to allow for a larger paved area. After all, space is valuable in a garden which measures 8 × 13 m (27 × 43 ft).

The half pond backs on to the supporting wall of the higher terrace next to the house. It is not visible at all when you first step onto the terrace from the conservatory and you only become aware of it when you start to descend the steps which are positioned either side of it. A stone lion-mask wall-fountain gently dribbles into the water below.

Both fountains are electrically driven by submersible pumps which are operated by switches in the house.

I am a modest man but I did a very good job here.

Two water features in a brand new garden provide distraction from the still immature plants.

3

INNOVATIVE WATER GARDENS

Water has always fascinated man.

It is always fun to experiment with it and to see how far we can stretch its versatility. Sir Geoffrey Jellicoe C.B.E. could be described as the best-known contemporary exponent of this art. He has achieved interesting effects at Sutton Place (see p.64), perhaps best known as the home of the late Paul Getty. There are some other examples of his work at a house in Wiltshire. There, he developed various abstract shapes as he believes that, from an architectural point of view, perfectly straight lines 'drive the eye mad'. He also had Moslem architectural law in mind which says that nothing must be perfect as it is an insult to God, hence the abstract shapes. There are also water ripples in the centre of each of the lower pools of the cascade which illustrates the Mogul influence. They were the first to use this method in which water tries to find its own level.

I was particularly interested in his 'harmonic chords', which produce different 'notes' as water flows over them. They form a part of a series of cascades interlinking five small, matching ponds. They consist of copper slithers set into concrete. The idea is that their different undulating shapes produce accordingly different water noises as the water falls. These two copper chutes are followed by a straight piece of wood which produces a clear sheet of water, and a different 'note' again.

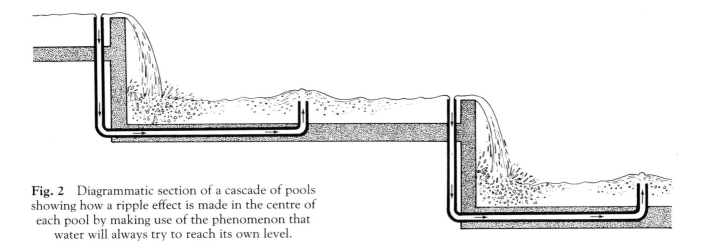

Fig. 2 Diagrammatic section of a cascade of pools showing how a ripple effect is made in the centre of each pool by making use of the phenomenon that water will always try to reach its own level.

(Opposite) An iwan at the end of a small canal with an aqueduct on the left – two of many water features hand-built by the owner (see 'A Politician's Garden', page 68).

Water which is encouraged to flow thinly over specially etched or chiselled surfaces can produce interesting, rippled patterns. This method was adopted by the Moguls on the rocky hillsides that descend to the waters of Lake Dal. This ingenious way of forcing flowing water to 'perform' is adopted too little nowadays.

The reflective properties of large expanses of water are often ignored. Sheffield Park should be in everyone's diary for a visit in the autumn, when the dazzling autumnal colouring looks as if it has had a mirror placed underneath it on a sunny, still day. Ben Nicholson's wall at Sutton Place is a superb example, where his magnificent, white-marble wall-sculpture shimmers as it is reflected – interrupted as it is by the occasional waterlily.

Water is fascinating stuff, whether it is seen splashing, sparkling, reflecting, making music, used for floating, forming patterns, or frozen.

Coupled with its many practical uses, we simply could not survive without it.

Aquatic Surprises in Oxfordshire

Here we see a cascade gushing from under the back of a Swiss chalet. On its other side is an artificially built, nineteenth-century lake. By pulling out a plug near to the lake's water surface, the cascade bursts into life and the water crashes down towards a pond surrounded by a forest of giant cow parsnip (*Heracleum giganteum*).

Written on the back of a bench in front of the Swiss chalet overlooking the lake towards the house is written:

The kiss of the sun for pardon.
The song of the birds for mirth.
One is nearer God's heart in the garden
than anywhere else on earth.

The swimming pool was completed quite recently. The owner built it having first construc-ted the steps which lead up to it from the orangery. Its maximum depth is 2·1 m (7 ft) and it is partially heated by solar panels which are tucked away out of sight down one side. Two magnificent Elizabethan wyverns stand guard, looking out onto the village whose roofs can be seen down below in the distance.

Walking down the steps from the swimming pool you see a round pond with a semi-submerged bust of a British general in the centre. Behind it is the orangery and to the sides are curved stone seats and ornamental stone urns. This spot has a special feel about it, perhaps because it is surrounded by mature hedges which make one feel secure.

Throughout the garden, white doves which have been dyed yellow, red, or 'any colour that comes to hand', strut about with total indifference to the visitor.

(Opposite) A forest of giant cow parsnip (*Heracleum giganteum*) stands guard around a pond, while water gushes from under a Swiss chalet.

THE ROOF GARDEN AT 99 KENSINGTON HIGH STREET, LONDON

This 1½ acre roof garden, over 30 m (100 ft) high, is unique. From up here you can see a panoramic view of London, with the dome of St Paul's on the skyline.

There are several different gardens here including the Spanish Garden, the Tudor Courts and the Old English Garden. There is also a waterfall and stream which is perhaps the most difficult to imagine on a roof of this altitude. There are some fine large specimen trees around and about – their very size dumbfounds the visitors. They are all protected by tree preservation orders and are thought to be the only trees (certainly in the UK) in such a location to be protected in this way. They are regularly root-pruned so that they do not grow *too* large. The gardens took three years to build, to the design of the landscape architect Mr Ralph Hancock, and under the direction of Mr Trevor Bowen, who was at that time Chairman of Barkers Ltd. The gardens were completed in 1938. The average soil depth is around 60 cm (2 ft), on a brick and clinker drainage system. As the goodness in the soil is continuously being washed away, it has to be added to annually to keep it alive and fresh. This is achieved with tonnes of organic matter.

The actual positioning of the plants had to be carefully considered bearing in mind the freak squalls that are sometimes caused in some parts of the garden, owing to the fact that winds do funny things at this altitude by rebounding off neighbouring buildings. The winter winds are very cold, but these are partly compensated for by the warm air which comes up from the department store underneath.

The one great advantage of growing roses at this height is that aphids do not appear to fly much above 12 m (40 ft)!

The garden is, at present, owned by Virgin (of record fame) and it is the main attraction of the Garden Club.

Flamingoes preening themselves over 100 ft high up in the English garden above 99 Kensington High Street. *(Opposite)* Ralph Hancock's Spanish garden. Note the rill with the spire of St. Mary's church in background.

SUTTON PLACE, NEAR GUILDFORD, SURREY

Sutton Place is steeped in history and was one of the first manor houses built without defences. It was built in the 1520s for Sir Richard Weston; his son Francis was one of those beheaded by Henry VIII on trumped-up charges for apparently having been one of Anne Boleyn's lovers. The Weston family, who continued to live here for several generations afterwards, were rather impoverished which explains why the house was never 'modernized'. We are all grateful for their impecunity!

Nothing much was done to the grounds of Sutton Place landscape-wise until *circa* 1900 when Lady Northcliffe created the Great Terrace to the south of the house. This includes a magnificent yew hedge. In 1902, Gertrude Jekyll, who worked with Sir Edwin Lutyens on many gardens, came to Sutton and planned several planting schemes. Sadly, like so many of the other gardens she planned, nothing remains of her work. The several water features at Sutton Place are among many inimitable landscaping surprises in the most recent major landscaping undertaken there. These schemes were planned by Sir Geoffrey Jellicoe in 1980, and work commenced in 1981.

Sutton Place: One of the 'Six Ages of Man' masks in the Paradise Garden by Sir Geoffrey Jellicoe.

Here in the Paradise Garden – 'the concept of heaven brought to earth' – we see six masks set into the walls, three on each side. These masks are all different, each representing the ages of man. Each is 2·1 m (7 ft) from the ground and spouts water into large earthenware dishes, the water being driven by submersible pumps which are situated in underground plastic-lined tanks (Fig. 3). There are two pumps, each dealing with the three masks on either wall. The four central fountains share a third pump.

The Swimming Pool Garden contains one of the very earliest known swimming pools in the UK, which was built by the Duke of Sutherland in the 1930s. Sir Geoffrey, having been very impressed by one of Miro's paintings, was inspired to choose this particular shape for the raft, which is anchored to the bottom of the swimming pool. The round stepping-stones which lead towards the raft are supported on stout columns. I felt very much at peace with the world as I sat on my 1950s-shaped artist's palette pontoon.

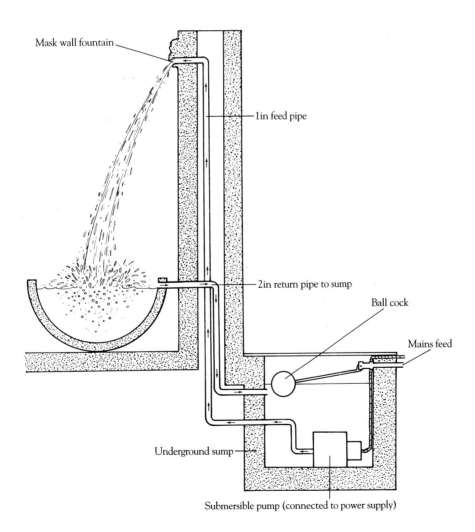

Mask wall fountain

1in feed pipe

2in return pipe to sump

Ball cock

Mains feed

Underground sump

Submersible pump (connected to power supply)

Fig. 3 Diagram showing how the wall mask fountains operate. In the average domestic situation, the submersible pump will be found in the bottom of the receptacle into which the water flows.

Myles Challis Esq of Leytonstone, London

This is the closest I have ever got to a jungle in the middle of East London! The vegetation is of an exotic nature, to say the least. Despite the omnipresence of eye-catching foliage plants, the hand emerging from the water at the end of the garden still succeeds in making its presence felt. It is large, but as it is surrounded by so many large-leaved plants it is in scale. This water sculpture symbolizes someone about to drown in a jungle swamp. They have just made one last desperate attempt to grab onto something. Unfortunately, it was a branch which snapped under their weight.

The planting includes *Aesculus indica*, *Catalpa × erubescens* 'Purpurea', *Corylus maxima* 'Purpurea', ('purple-leaved filbert'), *Polygonum cuspidatum* 'Spectabile' (syn. *P. sachalinense* 'Variegatum'). (The latter is a variegated variety of that dreaded pernicious weed introduced to this country by the Victorians from Japan during the last century as an ornamental plant. It has hollow stems, devilishly deep roots and is responsible for driving many a gardener insane.) Further planting includes the magnificent huge-leaved hosta (*H. sieboldiana* 'Elegans'), *Crambe cordifolia* (with a magnificent spray of tiny white flowers), Abyssinian banana (*Musa ensete*) and the rice paper plant (*Tetrapanax papyrifera*).

This garden is a guaranteed feast for a dedicated plantsman, or should we now correctly call ourselves 'plantspeople'?

A dramatic sculpture representing someone about to drown in a jungle swamp. Note how the figure appears to have made one last desperate attempt to grab onto a branch, which has then snapped under his weight.

A lush jungle in Leytonstone! Bold contrasting leaves surround the dainty sprays of white flowers of *Crambe cordifolia*.

A Politician's Garden in Gloucestershire

This garden was never planned, but rather, it evolved. It has taken 25 years to transform it from a rubbish tip, and it has all been done by one man on and off during weekends, weather permitting.

In fact, there are two gardens here, and both are linked by a series of waterways which are hand-dug channels fed by the local river, the Windrush. The round pond in the formal garden is fed by an underground pipe which emanates from the primula garden. The owner of this garden grows all his own primulas from seed, but occasionally finds he has to buy in new species from which he collects seed. There are very few other plants here except for 'some of the other more amusing marsh marigolds'.

Some of the species of primula to be found here are *P. sikkimensis* (sulphur-yellow), *P. inverewe* (bright red), *P. involucrata* (white), *P. pulverulenta* Bartley 'strain' (magenta), *P. aurantiaca* (bright orange). After a cruel winter, their numbers have been drastically reduced. There are many different species of willow dotted about including *Salix lanata*, the woolly willow. The larger-growing species are continually being removed when they get too large, as they take so much goodness out of the soil, and later replaced with new.

The round pond and bridge were the only two features in this garden planned to fit in with the architecture of the house. The canal, which contains about 30 rainbow trout, the iwan, and the greenhouse behind were all built by the owner of this garden, too. An iwan, incidentally, is usually to be found outside an Arabian house. It is really a porch where you sit and receive guests. This one is all hand-cut of local sandstone with a hammer and chisel.

Looking now from the round pond you will see, on the left, a stone urn. This is fed with water by a pump from the canal which in turn feeds the aquaduct. Near to the iwan, the water branches off into three directions: one heads into the primula water garden, one travels into the greenhouse and the last moves off to the right, through the hedge into a water butt.

I especially liked this garden as it is the result of one man's imagination. Slugs and snails also like it, especially the primulas, revelling in the damp conditions. Their numbers are kept down by slug traps containing beer.

The several waterways make weeding much less of a chore. The weeds are simply thrown into the water and the current does the rest.

(Opposite) Primulas and geraniums form a brightly coloured foreground for the stream and water-surrounded island beds beyond.

4

WATER GARDEN PLANTS

There is no doubt that a plain stretch of water is enhanced by water-loving plants. However, I would think twice before meddling with the banks of Lancelot Brown's lake at Blenheim Palace. It needs no further embellishment. Even messy old Queen Elizabeth Island fits in perfectly with the 'natural' landscape (see p.28). The average-size, informal garden pond can afford quite a bit of planting but you must be careful at the same time not to overcrowd it.

Perhaps, you have to be even more careful with small formal ponds. (In any case be very careful with their design – they can so easily look bland and square.) I can see architectural plants with dramatic sword-like leaves stabbing the air (e.g. *Iris* spp especially *Iris laevigata* 'Variegata' with white- and green-striped leaves and handsome purple flowers), or the graceful wands of *Cyperus alternifolius* playing a merry dance in the breeze, even a clump of waterlily (*Nymphaea* spp) towards the centre of the water rather than a clump of marsh marigold (*Caltha palustris*).

The test of a good eye is the laying out of a Japanese water garden, where only a few, specially chosen plants are required. As the choice is limited for the most part to those with exceptionally interesting shape, perhaps the job is made easier as you have fewer to choose from. (See Chapter 5.)

Water plants should be in scale with their surroundings. For example, the massive leaves and flowers of *Gunnera manicata* would overwhelm a small pond, whereas they always complement the shores of a lake. In the same way, the diminutive water lily *Nymphaea pygmaea* should not be encouraged to venture further than the compound of a barrel water garden. Many water-loving plants can become too invasive for comfort. If given a free rein they can easily choke all other inmates. Those innocent-looking sprigs you bring home from the garden centre can eventually prove to be a real nuisance, one example being the tiny water soldier (*Stratiotes aloides*) which can choke a small pond in no time.

Nearly all water-loving plants are propagated by division, although some genera, for example *Orontium*, are easily raised from seed in pots set in shallow water. Bog plants are also best propagated by division during mid spring, just as the new fresh growth is beginning to emerge.

Before you stock your pond, use the winter to read up about suitable plants. After all, spring is the time to plant them.

(Opposite) Here in the snake pool at Sezincote a snake wraps itself around the central Yew trunk, surrounded by yellow-flowering *Primula florindae*.

Sezincote, Moreton-in-Marsh, Gloucestershire

This lovely garden lies in a natural valley. As a result, little, if any, removal of soil was necessary during its layout. The early nineteenth-century planting acts as an excellent backdrop to the planting around the edges of the various streams and ponds. This site was originally an arboretum, as portrayed in contemporary pictures by Thomas Daniell.

It is known that Humphrey Repton was consulted about the layout of the garden by the then owner of Sezincote. A sketch exists by Repton showing his ideas for the South Garden. He also

The snake pool at Sezincote can be approached via stepping-stones under a bridge.

Surya, the Hindu God, presides over this pond at Sezincote. Note the predominantly grey planting.

mentions his work here in several of his writings, including those connected with his plans for the Brighton Pavilion. Apart from the one main spring which feeds the water gardens from a false cave at the top, there are several smaller springs which join it on its way down. The planting of the Thornery, or water garden, was rescued by Lady Kleinwort with the help of her adviser, Graham Thomas.

The top pool is presided over by Surya, a Hindu God mentioned in the Vedas, and he is seen here sitting in his little temple. Devout Hindus used to pray to him every day to stimulate their intellect. This makes a pleasant change from virility, but there is no escaping the subject of sex for long: the phallic properties of the fountain see to this. The planting around this delightful piece of water is predominantly grey and includes *Lonicera korolkowii* and grey-leaved rock roses (*Helianthemum* 'The Bride').

Following the stream one can see a wide selection of interesting plants, the masses of blue *Campanula lactiflora* being very much in evidence. There is also a Chilean bamboo (*Chusquea couleou*) as well as a weeping form of white mulberry (*Morus alba* 'Pendula'). There are large groups of *Hosta sieboldiana* 'Glauca', *Rodgersia podophylla* and *R. tabularis* hugging the side of the stream.

The Snake Pool is approached by crossing stepping-stones under the bridge. Here, there is a three-headed snake wrapped around a dead yew trunk. It was originally designed to wrap itself around a smooth pillar but this had not been delivered in time for a date in 1806 when the Prince Regent came to Sezincote from Ragley Hall for lunch. The estate workers were in such a hurry to get it finished in time that they forgot to connect it to the water supply. The story goes that the snakes were not spouting water because they so disapproved of the Prince's life style. Mind you, they were not working when *I* visited the garden, but I am told they only do so on special occasions. In and around the Snake Pool were masses of yellow flowers supplied by St John's wort (*Hypericum calycinum*) around the edge, and the Chinese cowslip (*Primula florindae*) around the centre.

Further down, via a series of small bridges, you arrive at the Rock Pool whose margin is dotted with assorted primulas. Beside the rocks is a mass planting of hydrangeas. Amongst them is *Hydrangea* 'Preziosa', a mop-head species with unusual red-blotched florets.

The very last pool of all before the water drains away, forgotten and unthanked for all the marvellous work that it has done, has a plain wooden bridge spanning it. From here, there are stunning views of the house, a unique example of the architecture of Akbar (a mixture of Hindu and Moslem). All the water gardens here reflect this style with an assortment of Eastern garden ornaments dotted all around them.

Burnby Hall, Packington, Yorkshire

The lakes at Burnby Hall were laid out by Major P. M. Stewart in 1904. The two lakes are lined with concrete – all 1½ acres of them. It cost £7000 to build and was originally intended for trout-fishing, with thick waterside planting acting as cover for anglers.

In around 1935, three-course-high, brick planting-beds of various sizes were built on the floor of the lakes and planted with varieties of waterlily. Originally, there were 52 varieties grown

here and it is still one of the largest collections in Europe.

Waterlilies (*Nymphaea* spp) flower over a long period from early summer to mid-autumn in the UK. Here, we can only grow hardy species, the tropicals only succeed in warmer climates. Hardy species will tolerate freezing conditions so long as the soil in which they are growing does not freeze solid. There is certainly no need for them to be molly-coddled. They vary enormously in size and

A magnificent display of waterlilies at Burnby Hall, which includes *Nymphaea* 'Conqueror' and *N.* 'Gladstoniana'.

are, therefore, planted at different depths. For example, *Nymphaea pygmaea* and varieties will grow in water 15 cm (6 in) deep (ideal for those limited for space), whereas *Nymphaea* 'Glad-stoniana', a vigorous species with huge white flowers is only suitable for lakes. Their flowers last almost exactly one week from the time they first appear as a bud. Their needs are relatively simple: they require ordinary soil but must have full sun and still water. They should annually be tidied up at the end of the season during early to mid-autumn before they die back and dirty the bottom of the pond. Fish and snails leave them alone, their main enemy being ducks which will sever their leaf- and flower-stems just for the sake of it.

If their leaves jut out of the water instead of lying flat, this is an indication that the plant needs thinning. This can also happen when a vigorous species has been planted in water that is too shallow for it.

They are best propagated by dividing their roots. Their rhizomes can also be cut up into pieces and placed in shallow water to start off with. It is advisable to handle waterlily roots with rubber gloves as they can stain badly, especially under the finger nails.

Soon after being planted, they have a tendency to float to the surface unless they are tied or pegged down. However, once their roots have got a firm grip on the soil they will stay put. They are best started off in shallow water and slowly introduced to greater depth, according to the species.

Finally, waterlilies help enormously with the well-being of their pond for one simple reason: they provide shade, thus discouraging the formation of algae.

GREAT DIXTER, NORTHIAM, EAST SUSSEX

The gardens at Great Dixter are laid out on the site of a farm. Many of the farm buildings were retained and now serve as an integral part of the landscape. The gardens surround a timbered house, parts of which date back to the fifteenth century.

The gardens here are supervised by Christopher Lloyd, who needs no introduction. It was his father, Nathaniel Lloyd, who bought the property and entrusted the design of most of the gardens to Edwin (later Sir Edwin) Lutyens, whose close professional working relationship with the landscape designer Gertrude Jekyll is legendary. This work was completed before the First World War. The Sunk Garden, a later addition, was designed by Nathaniel Lloyd, and the planting around today reflects Christopher Lloyd's know-ledge of plants. The splendid *Eryngium giganteum*, a statuesque sea holly, stands sentinel all around. The vivid splashes of red are supplied by *Crocosmia* 'Lucifer'. Other plants include *Phlox paniculata*, *Coreopsis verticillata*, *Erigeron mucronatus* (growing in the walls), as well as a number of ornamental grasses. Out of sight, behind the photograph as it were, there was a morello cherry growing up against a north-facing wall, laden with the weight of fruit and well netted against the birds.

The octagonal pond in the centre is lined with Butyl and planted up with 'Blue Beauty' and 'Rose Arey' waterlilies. 'Blue Beauty' is, in fact, a tropical species. Here, it is growing in its own container connected to a thermostatically-controlled immersion heater!

The other water plants here are *Iris laevigata*, *Iris* 'Gerald Darby', and the submerged water soldier (*Stratiotes aloides*).

(Opposite) The Sunk Pool at Great Dixter. The waterlily *Nymphaea* 'Blue Beauty' is a tropical species kept warm during the winter using a thermostatically-controlled immersion heater!

A lilac arch frames the entrance to the round pond at Hidcote Manor.

HIDCOTE MANOR, GLOUCESTERSHIRE

Considering this garden was once described as the best in England by Vita Sackville-West, it is somewhat surprising that no diaries of document-ation of any sort concerning the planting or con-struction of the garden exist today. It was only started in 1907, by Major Lawrence Johnston. In 1948, he handed it over to the National Trust.

Hidcote sits in a rather exposed position on a thin, chalky soil, so it was unexpected that anyone thought of creating a garden on such a large scale. Walking around the 10-acre garden here is a positive delight. It consists of a series of different gardens separated by hedges. It is just like walking through rooms in a house; indeed, it was once described as looking down onto a house without a roof.

The first water feature you come across is viewed through a 'door' in a hedge with another 'door' stretching the vista on further. Beyond, is the Mirror Pool. Originally, it was much smaller, a mere slice of what it is today, and it was level with the ground. Later, it was built up and it almost takes over this particular garden completely, the idea being that it should become a mirror pool to

Lush waterside planting showing *Rodgersia aesculifolia* to the left, the lush leaves of *Lysichitum camtschatcensis* in the centre and purple-flowering *Primula florindae* in the foreground.

reflect the overhanging trees (including a pair of *Magnolia soulangiana*, of which only one exists today) and the sky. Almost every winter this pool suffers from damage as it only has a stone base with a concrete rendering. Every attempt has been made to rectify this problem. For example, it was painted with an epoxy resin which, it was hoped, would not only fill in the cracks but also give it elasticity to enable some movement. At one stage, it was suggested that the mirroring effect would be vastly improved if the bottom of the pool were painted black. However, it was left a more neutral and natural colour.

There are informal water features further along into the garden. Here we see *Rodgersia aesculifolia*, two comfreys, *Symphytum uplandicum* (with deep-blue flowers) and *Symphytum* 'Hidcote Blue' with very pale, blue flowers. Also to be seen are the shuttlecock fern (*Matteuccia germanica*), purple-flowering candelabra primula (*P. florindae*), *Lysichitums*, *Tsuga canadensis* (the weeping conifer on the other side of the stream), and a rather battered-looking butcher's broom (*Ruscus aculeatus*) near to the bridge.

From the bridge looking downstream, the positions of the plants have been chosen according to their colour. That is to say, the flowers of plants near to the bridge have warm colours (reds and oranges) whereas those further downstream have cool colours (whites and blues). These cool colours start to appear where the garden becomes more shaded.

THE ROYAL HORTICULTURAL GARDENS AT WISLEY, SURREY

The Royal Horticultural Society's garden at Wisley was originally owned by George F. Wilson who farmed at Weybridge and, during the 1870s, purchased 60 acres at Wisley to use as an informal and experimental garden. Upon Wilson's death in 1903, the estate was purchased by Sir Thomas Hanbury (creator of the world famous gardens at La Mortola in Northern Italy) and given in trust to the Royal Horticultural Society for their perpetual use as an experimental and educational garden.

The magnificent rock garden was completed in 1911. Over the past 80 years the Society has developed one of the finest display gardens in the world, carefully planned to be attractive and interesting all the year round.

The garden lies alongside the main London to Portsmouth Road (A 3), some forty minutes from the centre of London. It is open daily from 10 am (except on Sundays when it opens at 2 pm) until 7 pm, or sunset, according to the season.

(Opposite) Wisley: Ducks are fed by visitors at a pond below the great rock garden completed in 1911.

Trollius europaeus in the foreground with azaleas beyond demonstrate rich waterside planting at Wisley.

BETH CHATTO OF ELMSTEAD MARKET, ESSEX

Twenty-six years ago the site on which this house and garden sits was wasteland situated between two farms near Elmstead Market, in the depths of the Essex countryside. The land is sloped. The higher reaches of it take the form of a six-acre, dry, gravel bank which gets hot and sunny during the summer and which, of course, drains in a flash – 'water runs through it like a colander'. Up here, alpines and other plants which like these sorts of conditions are grown. This is known as the Mediterranean Garden.

The lower part of the garden used to be a large soggy ditch fed by a spring – 'even cows were up to their middles in it'. This has been transformed into a charming series of ponds where the visitor can see a wide selection of water-loving plants for both sun and shade.

There are also wide aprons of interesting

Interesting leaf variations at Beth Chatto's garden in spring.

plants under trees in other parts of the garden. The entire garden has a neat appearance about it without looking too groomed. There is a decided lack of weeds. This effect is achieved by very close planting and regular mulching. 'This would make very fussy weeding if it wasn't for the way we plant'.

Although this garden is open to the public, Beth Chatto, its creator, feels that it is 'still very much my private garden'. She has now been a Gold Medal winner at Chelsea Flower Show several times over, and is also a very successful author. Her nursery which adjoins her garden contains a wide selection of mouth-watering plants, as listed in her booklet *Unusual Plants*.

Beth Chatto's enthusiasm for her plants really sparkles through. You will find all sorts of less commonplace species of plant here.

The giant leaves of *Gunnera manicata* dwarf the children kneeling beside it in Beth Chatto's garden.

LONGSTOCK PARK, NEAR STOCKBRIDGE, HAMPSHIRE

This garden used to be an apple orchard 50 years ago. The underlying gravel was dug up to make the nearby road, and the workings were later flooded by digging a connecting channel to them from the nearby river. The site became a water garden, as such, during the 1950s when further channels and lagoons were excavated and Perrys planned the planting. Other areas of the garden are still being developed. The gardens are owned by the John Lewis Partnership.

The entrance into this garden is through a tunnel of bamboo. The walk so far is without charm so it comes as quite a surprise to see this beautiful water garden suddenly before you.

The water gardens at Longstock contain a glorious selection of water-loving plants within a woodland setting.

Longstock: The dramatic flowers of *Rheum palmatum* in the distance are perfectly landscaped, with a colourful display of primulas in the foreground.

Longstock: The thatched summer-house provides an excellent spot in which to sit and admire one's surroundings.

The whole garden is almost entirely surrounded by mature woodland. There are some interesting trees within it too, mostly poplar, ash, oak, as well as swamp sypress (*Taxodium distichum*) and *Liquidamber formosana monticola*.

All the lagoons are surrounded, for the most part, by rich and varied planting, although the wide lawn-paths which meander throughout the garden do dip down into the water's edge here and there. Plain, plank bridges span watercourses to offer the visitor a different route.

There is a very wide selection of water lilies here, but I visited the garden too early in the year to appreciate them. However, the earliest to flower here is *Nymphaea virginale*, which was ready to burst when I visited the garden in early summer.

5

JAPANESE WATER GARDENS

The history of Japanese gardening goes back to around the third century AD. The Japanese were at first strongly influenced by Indian and Chinese cultures, after which Zen Buddhist priests were largely responsible for developing a style of their own. Their original design was very much controlled by a mixture of superstition, tradition and symbolism of Zen Buddhism. The main aim was to create a place for quiet meditation.

Raked gravel surrounding a carefully chosen and positioned rock is often used in this style of gardening. The rock becomes a mountain and the gravel represents sea – or 'water in dry landscape'. This style may appear stark to some, in which case actual water can always be used. Many found that they were squeezed for space and as a result had to resort to miniaturization of plants, or bonsai (the literal translation is 'grown in a tray').

In Japanese gardening, the Japanese portray many different scenes, both mythical and factual, but always in harmony with nature. Every single item – whether plant, lantern or stone, – is carefully placed for a purpose. Flowers play an insignificant part in the overall design. The plants and trees are considered the most important features, as they are permanent. There should always be a high percentage of foliage. No one feature is complete in itself; it always has near to it plants, stones or lanterns.

The success of the design and layout of a Japanese garden can be judged by the quality of overall peace and tranquillity. It must also have a strong sense of belonging to nature.

It was during the 1860s that Japan's ports were opened again, having been closed to travellers for several centuries. As a result, there exploded throughout Europe a vogue for everything Japanese, including gardens. The most authentic ones were built by workforces brought over from Japan for expressly that purpose.

(Opposite) The Japanese Garden at Compton Acres. Note the lead heron acting as decoy to protect the valuable orfe and koi.

Compton Acres, near Bournemouth, Dorset

The gardens at Compton Acres were planned and built by an architect, a Mr Thomas Simpson, soon after the First World War. Even in those days the work cost £220 000. This represents approximately £3 000 000 today. Rough moorland was transformed into a series of gardens, all three of them – the Italian Garden, the Water Garden and the Japanese Garden – are laid out with a heavy accent on water. The gardens are still privately owned today. They are immaculately kept up with only six gardeners.

I was shown round by the Head Gardener, Mr

A Torro gate at Compton Acres with dragons and doves representing the opposite powers of evil and good.

The Japanese garden at Compton Acres showing the tea-house covered in wisteria yet to bloom.

Collings, who has worked there for 23 years. When you first enter the gardens you are unaware of all the surprises you are about to encounter as each garden is not visible from the others. There is a strong feeling of surprise and mystery in the air. The soil excavated for the several ponds throughout the gardens was used to make the high banks that separate the individual gardens.

After the very formal Italian Garden you enter the Water Garden. Here, several ponds at different levels are fed by a powerful circulating pump via a tank on lower ground. In the last 23 years this garden has been completely replanted five times.

This is a policy of the gardeners, so that the plants always look fresh, vigorous and young. No plant is ever allowed to become overgrown.

There are several words to describe the Japanese Garden but I'll settle for magnificent. It was very difficult to photograph, as there were breathtaking views from every angle one chose. There was a strong scent of *Viburnum carlesii* in the air. The pond is full of colourful fish: koi carp and golden orfe. I was sorry to have missed the wisteria on the tea house which must look ravishing, reflected in the water. This garden is situated on the south coast, benefiting from the milder winters.

Octopus-like vine branches climb a pergola pillar in the Japanese garden at Compton Acres.

A lovely spring setting at Heale House with the red Nikko bridge beyond.

HEALE HOUSE, NEAR SALISBURY, WILTSHIRE

The Japanese garden at Heale House, near Salisbury in Wiltshire was laid out late last century by The Honourable Louis Greville, upon his return from Japan where he had been attached to the British Embassy in Tokyo. He returned home with a marriage arch (which has sadly since disintegrated), a nikko bridge, and a tea house.

The four Japanese gardeners and craftsmen whom he also included in his luggage worked with him laying out an extensive and very detailed copy of a traditional Japanese garden. The rockeries and ponds bear a deep and almost religious significance.

This sort of extravagant behaviour does seem rather 'over the top' for these days, but less than a century ago it was considered quite the norm. My

93

great-grandfather did exactly the same thing, and even brought back a new, large, wooden-carved hall for his house in Guernsey. The last of the Japanese towers, which housed his servants, was blown up by the Nazis whilst they occupied the Channel Islands during the Second World War.

The tea house at Heale House is of a large size, the main room containing eight tatami mats, the measurements of which have remained unchanged over many centuries. The house is built of wood with sliding rice paper shutters and the whole building is put together with such ingenuity and cunning that there is no visible use of nails or conventional fixings. It stands over cunningly channelled streams from the River Avon which

cross under it giving unparalleled views up and down river on all four sides. The large magnolia between it and the bridge is *Magnolia soulangiana*. The smaller weeping cherry is *Prunus* 'Yoshino', and the larger *Prunus* 'Tai Haku'. The bridge and the tea house were already old when they were removed from their homeland, and are thought to have been made in 1850.

Among groups of *Rodgersia*, *Pulmonaria*, *Gunnera* and *Lysichitum* are dotted about such trees as *Acer palmatum*, *cercidiphyllum*, *liquidamber*, *Prunus* and *Malus*. Many of these support climbing and rambling roses. The unfurling bright green fronds of the shuttlecock fern (*Matteuccia germanica*) complete this picture of serenity.

Sliding rice-paper doors frame the view of the Nikko bridge and *Magnolia soulangiana*, at Heale House.

A Wiltshire scene illustrating a Japanese-style weeping-cherry *Prunus* 'Yoshino', arching gracefully down to the water.

MR AND MRS ROGER HOLT OF BARKWAY, HERTFORDSHIRE

Here is a charming, small, Japanese-style garden which measures only 6 × 3 m (20 × 10 ft). Over it stands a simple wooden pergola clothed in *Clematis montana* 'Rubens' with its lovely pink-tinged flowers.

The planting includes a selection of evergreens so that during the winter the colour scheme is cream, green and white. The black temple is silhouetted up against the strong yellow foliage of *Philadelphus coronarius* 'Aureus' and the Japanese maple in the foreground is *Acer palmatum* 'Aka Shigitatsu sawa'. Other plants include *Mahonia* × 'Charity', *Alchemilla mollis*, *Corylus avellana* 'Contorta' as well as a variety of hostas.

The most remarkable thing about this garden is its fountain. You are never likely to come across another quite so small! It consists of a small submersible pump sitting in the bottom of a plastic bucket. The bucket is lined with plastic sheeting which overlaps some distance from the bucket to catch and return the water which is thrown out by the pump. Over the top of the bucket is a perforated plastic lid. Both this and the plastic sheet are camouflaged by gravel and stones. The electric cable, which enables the pump to be turned on from inside the house, is also hidden from view.

This garden and its water feature is the ideal solution for those who have limited space.

A *Clematis montana* 'Rubens'-clad pergola frames perfectly this delightful small Japanese garden.

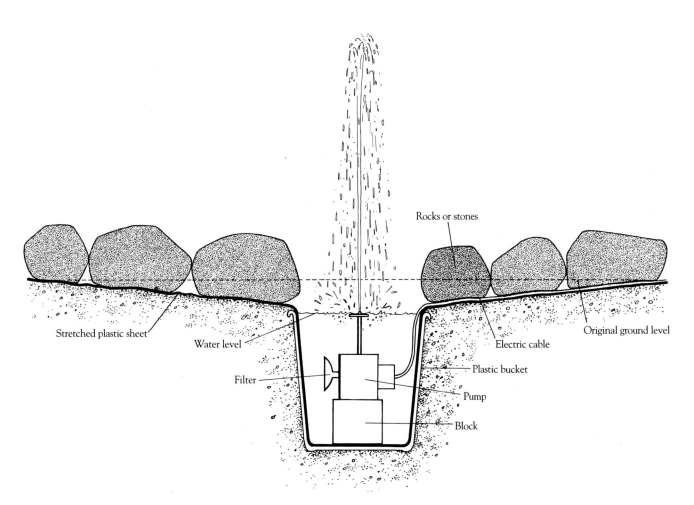

Fig. 4 Diagram showing how a simple fountain can be made by means of a small pump, polythene sheet and plastic bucket. Note that to ensure proper drainage of the water into the bucket, the area surrounding the bucket should be slightly excavated. In windy conditions, the plastic sheet will ensure that the water thrown wide by the fountain will percolate back into the bucket.

A pair of heron reflected in the water in the Japanese garden at Tatton Park.
(Opposite) A view towards the thatched tea-house in the Japanese garden at Tatton Park.

TATTON PARK, KNUTSFORD, CHESHIRE

The Japanese Garden at Tatton Park, Knutsford in Cheshire was built in about 1910 by Alan de Tatton Egerton (third Baron Egerton) with the help of a Japanese workforce specially brought over from Japan. The large Shinto temple was erected at the same time.

The design is typical of a 'rich lord's garden', with the thatched tea house being situated on the central feature, the Master's Island. Although the garden covers quite a small area, it has a feel of spaciousness about it. Every turn you make, you see a new perspective of this beautiful little garden. At one stage, you come across a large stone turtle squatting in a stream, acting as a stepping-stone.

The main eye-catcher is the tea house, but there are plenty more besides. I especially liked the miniature Mount Fuji, which is represented by a steep mound of soil capped with white 'snow stones'. Other special stones in the garden include

two which jut out into the stream: one is called the Stone of Easy Rest (*Ankio-seki*), which is traditionally the favourite sitting place of the Master; the other is the Stone of Amusement (*Yukio-seki*) and this is the Master's favourite spot for fishing. Then there is the Pagoda Viewing Stone whose purpose is self-explanatory.

The stone lantern on the curved stand is a Valley Lantern. A Snow Lantern stands where the streams join the lake; its elegant roof is designed to catch as much snow as possible so that it looks at its best when reflected in the water. The streams emerge from a bamboo glade.

The statuary includes deities such as Inari, the fox god.

Consistent with tradition, grass is not encouraged, in favour of moss.

This is indeed a very relaxing place, nestled as it is in among mature trees on most sides.

6

GROTTOES

'Another side, umbrageous Grots and Caves
Of coole recess, o'er which the mantling Vine
Layes forth her purple Grape....'
John Milton (1608–1674)

The dictionary definition of a grotto ia 'an imitation cave, usually fantastic'. Yes, it is certainly true that fantasy plays a large part in their make-up, which makes them all the more appealing. They are normally strongly associated with water and are, as such, purely ornamental extensions of the garden, although it has been mooted that they were originally used as retreats, for religious reasons.

It is recorded that grottoes were first being built during the seventeenth century, but it was not until 100 years later that they became lavish, and no expense was spared on them. Indeed 'in 1788 Lord Donegal had £10 000 of shells not yet unpacked'[1]. And further: 'When a house was put up for sale during the eighteenth century, a grotto was a good selling feature, as a swimming pool is today'.[1]

One of the grottoes I visited was in Twickenham, of all unlikely places. Of course, when it was built during the 1760s and 1770s it was surrounded by countryside. It consists of a labyrinth of subterranean rooms connected by long passages. It had special round channels which let in light and fresh air. It was built by a John Scott, and it is thought that he did so in order to escape any future epidemics of smallpox. His father and he had previously moved out of London in 1740 after the rest of the family had died from the disease.

As you will see these early grottoes were extravagantly embellished with shells, mineral crystals and semi-precious stones.

[1] *Follies & Grottoes*, Barbara Jones. Constable (1974).

Of Grotto's (John Woolridge, fl. 1669–98)[2]

'IT oftentimes happens that in these *Northern Climes*, the *AEstival* heats are more troublesome than they are nearer the *Zodiack*, the Sun continuing here longer above the *Horizon* in the Summer season, than in those parts, which occasions that intemperancy that many times we are sensible of, for as we have less of the presence of the Sun in the Winter, so have we that defect supplied in the Summer.

But those that inhabit more southerly, and have the Sun more perpendicularly over them, are more sensible of the acute heat of that bright Orb about the middle of the day, generally than we are, and therefore about the heat of the day, they usually sequester themselves from their ordinary occupations, and betake themselves to their shades and cool places of Recess for some few hours.

Such that have convenient places in their Villes, make themselves Grotto's or Caves in the Earth for that only purpose, on which some have bestowed so much cost and labour that those Grotts have been the object of admiration of, and part of the Subject of several Histories written by several Travellers and Strangers, as are their Baths and Fountains.

For the same reason may our Grotts be as necessary for us, to repose our selves in the time of our Summer faint heats, although they are not here so constant every year as in those parts, yet are they less tolerable, for want of these nocturnal breezes they usually enjoy.

Therefore either in the side of some declive of a Hill, or under some Mount or Terrace artificially raised, may you make a place of repose, cool and fresh in the greatest heats. It may be Arched over with stone or brick, and you may give it what light or entrance you please. You may make secret rooms and passages within it, and in the outer Room may you have all those before mentioned water-works, for your own or your friends divertisements.

It is a place that is capable of giving you so much pleasure and delight, that you may bestow not undeservedly what cost you please on it, by paving it with Marble or immuring it with Stone or Rock-work, either Natural or Artificially resembling the excellencies of nature. The Roof may be made of the same supported with pillars of Marble, and the partitions made of Tables of the same.

The most famous of this kind that this Kingdom affords, is that *Wiltonian Grotto* near unto *Salisbury*, on which no cost was spared to make it compleat, and wherein you may view or might have lately so done the best of waterworks...'

[2] From *Systema Horticultura* or the *Art of Gardening*, published for Thomas Burrell in 1677.

An Eighteenth Century Grotto in Berkshire

One of the joys of writing this book was visiting places like this. Inside the grotto it was as quiet as quiet can be. The only noise was the occasional interruption of a mother bird returning to sit on her eggs. Nests were everywhere; a well and truly trusted spot.

The exact history of this grotto is not certain but there is a strong belief that it was built during the 1740s to the design of the owner, a Daniel Agace. It is possible that the design was executed by Josiah Lane and other members of his family. Many other grottoes of this period are attributed to the Lanes.

There was an explosion of grotto-building during the seventeenth century. By the eighteenth century, it would appear, no self-respecting aristocrat would be without one.

In this grotto, which consists of several cham-

The stalactite-covered ceiling of a grotto with a view of the lake beyond.

The downward stab of felspar-smothered stalactites, interspersed with red marble chevrons.

bers, the walls and ceilings are not covered in shells. It is situated under a pile of huge rocks on one side of the lake in full view from the house. When I visited it, the mound was covered in yellow alyssum and purple aubrieta.

Inside, there are arches of huge flints. There are also trickling pools, fed straight from the lake. Here and there are dotted octagons and circles set in the pebble floor. Niches with seats appear at every turn.

These days, the lighting in the grotto consists of very lightweight fibreglass stones with an electric bulb in each. They throw out a perfect, subdued light. There are signs of more old-fashioned means of lighting such as flame torches. Blackened patches indicate where they once were.

The grot work here is the most exciting part of it. The stalactites and ceiling are smothered in felspar, interrupted by zig-zags of brown minerals and fragments of a reddish marble. The felspar is sometimes mixed with quartz crystals.

The stalactites appear to have been made of wooden cones smothered in plaster into which the felspar fingers were fixed. The grotto which looks out on to the lake has to be approached by a separate entrance. As it is lit by daylight it can be appreciated and studied even more closely. On its walls, among the felspar, are groups of amethyst and quartz crystals, as well as jet, fragments of mosaic, and other semi-precious miscellanea.

THE GOLDNEY GROTTO, BRISTOL UNIVERSITY

This glorious grotto was the creation of Thomas Goldney III (1696–1768). The son of a Quaker shipper and merchant, he inherited the house and grounds at Clifton, Bristol. It now belongs to Bristol University. The grotto took him 27 years to build, and was completed in 1764. The shells were probably brought back in merchant ships from America and the West Indies. The majority of the fossils and minerals are British. The water is now propelled by electric pump, but was originally pumped by a steam-operated 'fire engine'.

The door to the grotto is reached down a ramped path. As you near it the roar of the water within can be heard for the first time. The first thing you see is a lion couchant, with his lioness behind peering menacingly at you through the entrance of their den. To your right and left are two columns encrusted in sparkling mineral crystals,

and there is the occasional light or grille above through which daylight enters. Disappearing round a corner to your right leads a dark, mysterious passage, but your attention is drawn immediately to the roar of water and the intricate shell-work to your left. The walls of the chamber are furiously decorated with every kind of shell imaginable, at least that is the impression it gave to me, an ignorant conchologist. The eye is led further on to a reclining marble figure of Neptune seen at the end of a jagged stone tunnel. His right arm rests on an upturned urn, out of which water gushes. The torrent crashes and tumbles down the stone tunnel and eventually reaches a pool, having first had to spill from one giant clam into another.

This is certainly a dramatic place. It was also very cooling after the warm, humid, mid-summer air outside.

Detail of the grot work in the Thomas Goldney Grotto, Bristol University. Note how water drips from one clam shell to another *(bottom right)*, to the pond below.

Columns encrusted in sparkling mineral crystals frame the view onto Neptune beyond, via a shell-smothered chamber.

7

FEATURES

Here are a few more ideas of how to use water in the garden. The shape and size of your garden will dictate the proportions of your water feature. The possibilities are endless. I leave the rest to your imagination.

STAPELEY WATER GARDENS, NEAR NANTWICH, CHESHIRE

This water garden was completed just one month ago. In the photograph you can see a tall reed (*Scirpus albescens*), a young bamboo (*Arundinaria nitida*), and the larger group of hostas are *Hosta fortunei* 'Albopicta'. In the water is the charming little plant water crowfoot (*Ranunculus aquatilis*).

You will also see a charming yellow-flowering mimulus (*Mimulus luteus*) and, to the right, an ornamental blue grass (*Festuca ovina* 'Glauca').

This only goes to prove that a brand-new garden need not look bare during its first few weeks.

A valley lantern anchors a new Japanese garden where stones play an important role.

(*Opposite*) A bamboo pole feeds water onto a round stone in a Japanese water garden.

107

Mrs H. O'Dare of Lansdown, near Bath

Here is a matching set of raised beds, measuring 4 m (12½ ft) long and 1·5 m (5 ft) wide. The owner wanted water in her garden as well as a peat bed, hence their coming into the world. A lion spouts water into the pond with the help of a submersible pump, controllable from the house.

The depleted planting in the pond can be explained by the presence of the duck. These dear creatures have a charming habit of severing leaves and flowerbeds of waterlilies just under the surface of the water, apparently just for the fun of it.

The peat bed comes in very handy as this is a lime soil district. It is used for all sorts of things including cuttings . . . 'It all gets jammed into the peat bed. If it grows it gets potted; if not, it gets discarded.'

Suitable for a small garden, a twin pond and peat-filled bed.

Mr and Mrs Bonython of Chiswick, London

For a small garden, this is a pleasant and informal way of having water. The choice of plants is interesting inasmuch as they all have bold interesting leaves.

This will give you some idea of how a newly planted garden looks. Because the root systems of the plants are still relatively small, the leaf size is similarly affected.

I like the simple idea of three curved terracotta slates forming an effective waterfall. Here, the water is not circulated by a submersible pump. The water is turned on at the mains so that it slowly overflows, seeping into the beds all around when they start to look dry.

Note the tall flower of *Rheum palmatum*. In a few seasons' time this will be seen emerging from a mass of interestingly contrasting leaves, the flower spire a good 1·8 m (6 ft) tall.

A newly-planted pond in a small garden on the river Thames.

CHELSEA FLOWER SHOW

B & Q garden

The designer of this garden, Robert Whitelegg, has spent some time in remote regions of Britain such as the Yorkshire Dales and Snowdonia, and he has tried to encapsulate the feeling of these wild, remote places in the small area allotted to him at the Chelsea Flower Show. The result is a natural-looking stone outcrop which includes a gently gurgling stream.

There is a strong theme of low maintenance here. The chipped-bark mulch is designed to quell the majority of weeds, as is the gravel under the alpines.

The water is propelled with a one-horsepower submersible pump capable of circulating nearly 16 000 l (3500 g) of water per hour. In this case, the valve has been adjusted to regulate the flow so that only 4550 l (1000 g) is kept circulating per hour.

The pool is made of reinforced concrete so that it can support the terrific weight of the enormous Forest of Dean above. A flexible liner simply could not take the weight.

A natural-looking stone outcrop ready for the Chelsea Flower Show.

Woolworth Garden
(designed by David Stevens)
Here we see an unusual idea where water is seen gushing through a small hole in a sandstone rock. There is also a waterfall underneath. This double flow of water is achieved by drilling a hole in the rock and inserting a pipe through it. The other pipe splits off the main pump to throw the water over the chute.

At the back there is a wall mask fountain. These are often criticized, as the water spouting out of them can be too strong resulting in a noisy and unrestful splash. This can be overcome by regulating an adjustable valve on the pump.

A drilled stone dribbles water behind an ornamental waterfall in a garden at the Chelsea Flower Show.

111

Mrs B. George of Middleton-on-Sea, West Sussex

Here is a unique fountain which is basically a wheel-thrown sculpture consisting of three bowls in increasing sizes. Its overall height is 60 cm (24 in), the diameter of the bottom bowl being 44 cm (17½ in). The whole sculpture sits on an inverted bowl which is larger still. It was designed by Jean Clark and commissioned for this particular garden. The difference between this one and most other garden sculptures is that it is glazed. There are splashes of blue on the glaze to suggest reflection from the water below. (Garden sculptures are normally *un*glazed terracotta or other stoneware.) The intention of this sculpture was that the flow of water from one bowl to the next should appear to be an integral part of the sculpture itself.

The water is circulated by means of a submersible pump. The garden in which the fountain and pond sit is also interesting. It was designed by Mark Rumary and consists of a series of circles, one of the simplest of all shapes. As we all know, the simplest things in life are the best, and the layout of this garden certainly proves that point. As crazy paving goes, you can't get better than this: York stone with uniform joins throughout, 'controlled' with circular paviors (Ockley seconds).

The planting is only two years old and is designed for low maintenance. Here we see romneyas, silver-leaved phlomis and artemisias among many others. Note the standard wisteria, an all-too-seldom-used method of training this lovely plant which is only just starting to flower.

Wisteria is lowered to the water's edge at Iford Manor, a garden laid out by Harold Peto.

Iford Manor, Bradford-on-Avon, Wiltshire

This is a small part of a garden laid out by Harold Peto just before the First World War. Peto was a very accomplished landscape architect who believed that a garden should be a combination of architecture and plants. He wrote: 'Old buildings or fragments of masonry carry one's mind back to the past in a way that a garden of flowers only cannot do. Gardens that are too stony are equally unsatisfactory; it is the combination of the two in just proportion which is the most satisfactory.'

He was particularly attracted by the charm of old Italian gardens. This becomes obvious when one walks around this garden dotted as it is with columns, sarcophagi and even a cloister which was built to house more antique fragments.

I am not absolutely sure whether Peto may not have gone a little bit over the top. One does seem to trip over something with practically every step one takes. But then, the garden may have changed since his day.

(Opposite) A series of circles containing a circular pond show crazy-paving at its best!

113

Mrs Jean Clark of Long Melford, Suffolk

Here I found a fascinating idea for a series of planting modules for either indoors or out. It is ideal for a very small area like a balcony. It consists of single, double and treble brick-sized containers which can be arranged at the owner's whim. The water is kept circulating by means of a submersible pump, the pump itself being situated in the bottom 'water garden'.

The modules are unglazed, with oxides rubbed into roughened surfaces with a blue slip on the rims. The water containers are glazed black on the inside. This gives them extra depth.

As people become more sophisticated they are becoming a little tired of having *a* plant in *a* pot. Here we all have the possibility of having several plants, albeit those of a smaller habit, with moving water *and* water plants too. Furthermore, it is easy to change the plants around or add new ones.

An ingenious method of introducing a water garden with waterfalls to a balcony or very small garden.

A swimming pool and water garden in one, with the sides accommodating marginal aquatics.

LADY D'AVIGDOR GOLDSMID OF TUDELEY, NEAR TONBRIDGE, KENT

As a landscape architect, I am forever criticizing the design of the average swimming pool. There they sit, blue and sterile, with very little effort having been made to 'marry' them to their surroundings. Here we have a swimming pool (which doesn't look like one) and a water garden in one!

The pool is lined with brown mosaic. It is 18 m (60 ft) long – 'the right stretch' – 1·05 m (3½ ft)

deep at the shallow end, and 1·7 m (5 ft 9 in) at the deep end. A diving board was omitted on purpose, as they are seldom objects of beauty. There are narrow steps at each corner, also lined with brown mosaic so that they do not stand out in any way, which lead down into the water.

The owner was so keen that the swimming pool should not look like one that she positioned it next to the house so that there was no need for a 'bathing house'.

The side channels containing the water plants are exactly the same depth as the swimming pool. These were designed in this way in case future generations wanted to remove them in order to create more space for swimming.

Beyond, is the conservatory shaded against strong summer sun, and constructed against a building that had once been a laundry.

FEATURE FROM MR & MRS C. CAZANOVE'S GARDEN (SEE ALSO P.57)

Half ponds come in very useful in gardens where space is limited, as they fit snugly up against a wall. They can be bought from various manufacturers, complete with semi-rigid liners with shelves for marginal aquatics. These ponds are made of reconstituted cement and can be 'anti- quated' if requested. The mask, in this case a lion's mask, must be chased into the brick/stone work with the appropriate plumbing hidden from view. Water is recirculated by means of a submersible pump which sits on the bottom of the pond.

The half-pond; ideal for the very small garden.

A Happy Meeting of Software and Hardware

The huge leaves of *Gunnera manicata* make it one of the most dramatic of all the waterside/bog plants. It can be seen in this photograph framing a Japanese bridge beyond. The plant should be given protection during the winter. The easiest way to do this is simply to place its own leaves upside down on top of the plant's crown in autumn.

A bridge framed by *Gunnera manicata*.

8

PLANT LISTS

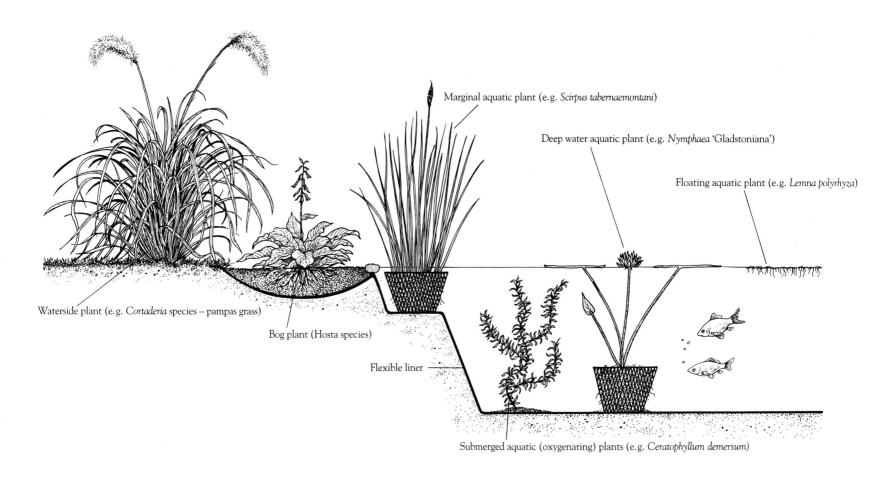

Marginal aquatic plant (e.g. *Scirpus tabernaemontani*)

Deep water aquatic plant (e.g. *Nymphaea* 'Gladstoniana')

Floating aquatic plant (e.g. *Lemna polyrhyza*)

Waterside plant (e.g. *Cortaderia* species – pampas grass)

Bog plant (Hosta species)

Flexible liner

Submerged aquatic (oxygenating) plants (e.g. *Ceratophyllum demersum*)

Fig. 5 Diagram to illustrate the different kinds of water-loving plants and their environment.

Here are plant lists which will enable the reader to plan his water garden depending on his requirements and needs.

A Selection of Trees and Shrubs Suitable for Planting at the Water's Edge

Botanic name	Common name (if any)	Comments
Alnus spp	alder	Good winter catkins. *A. incana* 'Aurea' has golden leaves and pink catkins.
Carpinus betulus	common hornbeam	Also excellent as hedging plant, its leaves being very similar to those of beech (*Fagus sylvatica*).
Cornus spp	dogwood	*C. alba* 'Sibirica' has bright red twigs throughout the winter. Tolerant of dry conditions too. Several other ornamental species.
Metasequoia glyptostroboides	dawn redwood	Fast growing. Easy to propagate from seed. Prefers to grow on water's edge. Shaggy, cinnamon-brown bark. Eventually grows very tall. Also tolerates dry conditions.
Populus spp	poplar	Very fast growing. *P. nigra* 'Italica' (Lombardy poplar) forms a quick, tall screen.
Populus tremula	aspen	Medium-sized. Tends to produce suckers. Wood used for match industry.
Salix daphnoides	willow	Several species including:
	violet willow	Yellow spring catkins. (height: 4·5–7·5 m; 15–25 ft)
S. lanata	woolly willow	Erect yellow catkins in spring. Silvery leaves. Slow-growing shrub (height: 0·6–1·2 m; 2–4 ft)
S. 'Wehrhahnii'		Dark purple-brown bark. White, woolly, spring catkins. (height: 1·2–1·5 m; 4–5 ft)
Taxodium distichum	swamp cypress	Most suitable conifer for wet soils. If planted at water's edge it will send 'knees' down into the water. Brilliant yellow autumn colour. Dislikes chalk. Will also tolerate dry conditions.

A Selection of Grasses for Wet Soils and Waterside Planting

Botanic name	Common name (if any)	Comments	Maximum height
Acorus gramineus 'Variegata'		Evergreen.	15–20 cm (6–8 in)
Carex morrowii 'Variegata'	sedge	Dwarf.	15 cm (6 in)
Cortaderia selloana	pampas grass	Very showy, silvery plumes.	1·8 m (6 ft)
Hakenochloa macra		Graceful and dainty.	15–20 cm (6–8 in)
Holcus mollis 'Variegata'	variegated Yorkshire fog		15–23 cm (6–9 in)
Miscanthus sinensis 'Zebrinus'	zebra-striped rush	Fascinating leaves marked with bands of pale yellow.	0·9–1·5 m (3–5 ft)
Phalaris arundinacea 'Picta'	gardener's garters	Good, bright variegation.	0·75 m (2½ ft)

A selection of Ferns for Waterside Planting

Botanic name	Common name (if any)	Comments	Maximum height
Matteuccia struthiopteris (syn. germanica)	shuttlecock fern ostrich feather fern	Best planted in groups. Spreads by underground rhizomes.	45–60 cm (1½–2 ft)
Onoclea sensibilis	sensitive fern	Spreads fast. Fronds turn brown at first frost – hence common name.	30–60 cm (1–2 ft)
Osmunda regalis	royal fern	Grows best where its roots can go down into water. It can help to stabilize banks.	1·2–1·5 m (4–5 ft)

A Selection of Plants for Boggy Soil

Botanic name	Common name (if any)	Flowers	Comments	Maximum height
Ajuga reptans	bugle	Blue. Early summer.	Fast-spreading ground cover. Purple-headed form is 'Atropurpurea'.	15 cm (6 in)
Alchemilla mollis	lady's mantle	Yellow/green. Early to late summer.	A wonderful plant to have anywhere in the garden.	30–45 cm (12–18 in)
Arum italicum 'Pictum'	lords and ladies	White.	Good winter foliage.	23 cm (9 in)
Astilbe spp	false goat's beard	Mostly white, red, pink. Mid-summer to mid-autumn.	A wide selection of species and hybrids, flowering from late spring to early autumn. Feathery foliage. Thrive in sun or shade.	30–90 cm (1–3 ft)
Bergenia spp	elephant's ears	Pinks, purples and reds. Early to mid-spring or summer.	Rounded, leathery leaves often evergreen, especially during mild winters. Thrive in sun or shade. Excellent ground cover.	30–45 cm (12–18 in)
Brunnera macrophylla		Bright blue. Late spring to early summer.	Good ground cover. Will tolerate dry conditions, resulting in smaller leaves, which are heart-shaped.	30–45 cm (12–18 in)
Campanula lactiflora	harebell; Canterbury bells	Blue. Mid-summer onwards.	'Prichard's Variety' is a very good blue.	0·9 m (3 ft)
Cimicifuga spp	bugbane	White. Mid-summer to early autumn.	Several species with striking foliage and wand-like flower spikes.	0·9–1·8 m (3–6ft)
Eupatorium cannabinum	hemp agrimony	Pink. Mid-summer to early autumn.	Commonly seen growing wild.	0·9 m (3 ft)
Euphorbia palustris	spurge	Sulphur yellow. Early to mid-summer.	Forms large clumps.	0·9 m (3 ft)
Filipendula palmata (syn. *Spiraea digitata*)		Pink. Mid-summer	Fluffy heads of flowers good for picking. Other species too.	60 cm (2 ft)
Gentiana asclepiadea	willow gentian	Blue/white. Late summer.	Shade-tolerant. Self-seeding.	37 cm (15 in)
Gentiana pneumonanthe	marsh gentian	Blue (varying shades). Late summer to early autumn.	Easily grown from seed.	15–23 cm (6–9 in)
Gunnera manicata	prickly rhubarb	Green, cone-shaped. Mid- to late spring.	Vast leaves which can be as wide as 3 m (10 ft) across and 3 m (10 ft) tall. Crowns must be protected in the winter.	2—3 m (6–10 ft)

In foreground Iris species, with *Lysichitum americanum* beyond. *Cornus florida* 'Rubra' in background.

A Selection of Plants for Boggy Soil – *continued*

Hemerocallis spp	day lily	Wide colour range. Mid- to late summer.	Very good value. Trouble-free, long-lived. Luscious foliage.	60–90 cm (2–3 ft)
Heracleum giganteum	giant hogweed	White. Mid- to late summer.	Huge and dramatic. Can cause skin rash.	2·4–3·6 m (8–12 ft)
Hosta spp	plantain lily	White and shades of lilac. Mid- to late summer.	Chiefly grown for lovely foliage. Shade-tolerant. Will also tolerate dry conditions. Several varying species.	0·6 cm–1 m (2–3 ft)
Iris (several) including *I. sibirica* 'Perry Pigmy'		Blue. Early summer.	Dwarf.	45 cm (1½ ft)
Iris foetidissima	gladwin iris	Purple. Early summer.	Shiny, green leaves and bright, orange seed pods during the winter.	37–45 cm (15–18 in)
Iris kaempferi cultivars	clematis iris	Wide colour range.	Revels in acid soils.	45–60 cm (1½–2 ft)
Ligularia dentata		Yellow/orange. Early to mid-summer.	Many species and cultivars.	0·9–1·5 m (3–5 ft)
Lobelia cardinalis		Rich red. Mid- to late summer.	Purple leaf and stem.	60 cm (2 ft)
Luzula nivea	white woodsedge			37 cm (15 in)
Lysichitum americanum	skunk cabbage	Yellow. Early spring	Arum-like flowers and huge Leaves (90 cm [3 ft] or longer). *L. kamtschatense* smaller, with white flowers.	1·2 m (4 ft)
Lysimachia nummularia 'Aurea'	creeping Jenny	Yellow. Early to mid-summer.	Evergreen, trailing and good ground cover. Attractive golden foliage. Also tolerant of dry soils.	15 cm (6 in)
Lysimachia punctata	yellow loosestrife	Yellow. Mid-summer.	Preferred to *L. vulgaris* which tends to become too invasive.	60 cm (2 ft)
Meconopsis betonicifolia	Himalayan blue poppy	Blue. Early summer.	A lime hater! Also M. *cambrica* (Welsh poppy); yellow flowers.	1·2 m (4 ft)
Mimulus cardinalis		Red. Early summer to early autumn.	Forms a neat clump.	60 cm (2ft)
Mimulus luteus	monkey musk	Yellow. Late spring to late summer	Avoid invasive spp, e.g. M. *guttatus*.	60 cm (2 ft)
Peltiphyllum peltatum	umbrella plant	Pink. Summer.	Striking autumn colour. 'Nanum' is a useful dwarf cultivar where space is limited.	1·5 m (4½ ft)
Physostegia virginiana	obedient plant	Pink/mauve. Late summer to early autumn.	If flowers are repositioned, they stay put – hence common name.	45–60 cm (1½–2 ft)

A Selection of Plants for Boggy Soil – *continued*

Polygonum affine 'Darjeeling Red'		Red. Mid-summer to early autumn.	Quickly forms a dense mat. Will also grow in dry conditions.	15 cm (6 in)
Polygonum amplexicaule	knotweed	Deep red. Mid-summer.	Hardy and useful ground cover.	45 cm (1½ ft)
Primula denticulata	drumstick primula	Wide colour range.	Strong growing; early-flowering.	15–23 cm (6–9 in)
Primula florindae	Chinese cowslip	Yellow. Early to mid-summer.	Sometimes called the 'giant cowslip'.	1·2–1·5 m (4–5 ft)
Primula japonica	candelabra primula	Magenta. Late spring to early summer.	Other candelabra primulas include *P. bulleyana* (orange, early/mid-summer); *P. aurantiaca* (Yellow/orange, early/mid-summer). Many others.	30–90 cm (1–3 ft)
Primula rosea		Rose-pink. Mid-spring.	Compact, tuft-forming.	10–15 cm (4–6 in)
Primula sikkimensis	Himalayan cowslip	Yellow. Early to mid-summer.	Fragrant flowers.	45 cm (18 in)
Rheum palmatum 'Rubrum'	ornamental rhubarb	Red. Early summer.	Large, rhubarb-like, purplish leaves. Flowers large, astilbe-like.	1·8 m (6 ft)
Rodgersia aesculifolia		White or pink. Mid-summer.	Splendid, bronzed, horse-chestnut-like leaves. Flowers like plumes.	0·9 m (3 ft)
Saxifraga fortunei		White. Mid-autumn.	Dainty flowers.	15–20 cm (6–8 in)
Schizostylis coccinea	kaffir lily	Scarlet. Mid- to late autumn.	Very useful for its late flowering S.c. 'Viscountess Byng' is pale pink.	60 cm (2 ft)
Spiraea digitata nana	meadowsweet	Pink.	Dwarf.	23 cm (9 in)
Thalictrum flavum glaucum	meadow-rue	Yellow. Mid- to late summer,		1·2 m (4 ft)
Tiarella cordifolia	foam flower	White. Late spring to early summer.	Quickly spreads to form a dense mat.	15 cm (6 in)
Tradescantia virginiana	spiderwort/trinity flower	Blue/pink/purple/white. Early summer to early autumn.	Hardy. Pointed, strap-like leaves.	30–45 cm (12–18 in)
Trollius europaeus	globe flower	Shades of yellow. Late spring to early summer.	Many cultivars and hybrids.	30–45 cm (1–1½ ft)
Zantedeschia aethiopica	arum lily	White.	This is the hardiest species which will only succeed out of doors in milder areas of the UK.	30 cm (1 ft)

A Selection of Hardy Marginal Aquatics

For very shallow water, up to 5 cm (2 in) in depth.

Botanic name	Common name	Flowers	Comments	Maximum height
Caltha palustris	marsh marigold	Yellow. Mid-spring.	*C.p.* 'Plena' is the double-flowered variety which often produces flowers again during late summer. *C.p.* 'Alba' has white flowers.	30 cm (12 in)
Cardamine pratensis	lady's smock	Pale purple. Mid-spring.	Tends to be invasive. *C.p.* 'Flore Pleno' is less so.	45 cm (18 in)
Iris laevigata	Japanese iris	Blue. Early summer.	Numerous varieties available.	60–75 cm (2–2½ ft)
Lythrum virgatum 'Rose Queen'	purple loosestrife	Pink/purple. Late summer.	Suited to a small pond.	45–60 cm (1½–2 ft)
Myosotis palustris	water forget-me-not	Blue. Early summer onwards.	Spreads fast. Excess growth is easily removed.	23–30 cm (9–12 in)

A colourful selection of water-loving plants at Wisley.

125

A Selection of Hardy Marginal Aquatics
For water 5–15 cm (2–6 in) in depth

Botanic name	Common name	Flowers	Comments	Maximum Height
Acorus gramineus 'Variegatus'	sweet flag	Rarely flowers	Evergreen, with white-striped leaves.	30 cm (12 in)
Calla palustris	bog arum	Arum-like. Mid- to late summer.	Grass-like foliage. Good for disguising pond edges.	10–13 cm (4–5 in)
Eriophorum angustifolium	common cotton grass	White. Late summer	Silky cotton-like flowers.	15–45 cm (6–18 in)
Iris pseudacorus	yellow flag iris	Yellow. Late spring/early summer	Also *I.p.* 'Variegata', which has golden leaf markings during early summer.	7–8 cm (3–3½ in)
Iris versicolor		Purple. Late spring	This will eventually outgrow a small pond.	45–60 cm (1½–2 ft)
Juncus	rush		Many different species. *J. effesus* 'Spiralis' (corkscrew rush) is an amusing variety.	45 cm (1½ ft)
Mentha aquatica	water mint	Lavender	aromatic leaves.	30 cm (1 ft)
Ranunculus lingua	spearwort	Yellow. Mid-summer onwards	flowers buttercup-like.	60–90 cm (2–3 ft)
Typha minima	reed-mace		Ideal for small ponds.	30–60 cm (1–2 ft)

A Selection of Hardy Marginal Aquatics
for water with max depth of 15 cm (6 in)

Botanic name	Common name	Flowers	Comments	Maximum height
Cyperus longus	English galingale		Hardy to light frosts only. Popular with the flower arranger.	45–48 cm (18–20 in)
Glyceria aquatica 'Variegata' (syn. 'Spectabilis')	sweet grass		Very attractive foliage, especially when young.	45–60 cm (1½–2 ft)
Menyanthes trifoliata	bog bean; buck bean	White. Late spring.	Good for disguising artificial pond edges.	30 cm (1 ft)
Orontium aquaticum	golden club	White. Late spring.	Waxy leaves. This plant must have full sun.	23–25 cm (9–10 in)
Pontederia cordata	pickerel weed	Blue. Late summer.	Neat in habit. Not invasive.	60—75 cm (2–2½ ft)
Sagittaria sagittifolia	European arrowhead	White. Summer.	Arrow-shaped leaves.	36–45 cm (15–18 in)
Scirpus	bulrush		Can become invasive.	1–2·5 m (3–8 ft)

A Selection of Hardy Oxygenating Plants

Botanic name	Common name (if any)	Flowers	Comments
Callitriche hermaphroditica	water starwort	Insignificant.	Good oxygenator. Leaves bunch to form starry masses on water surface. Several species.
Ceratophyllum demersum	hornwort		Brittle stems break off quite easily and root separately.
Chara spp	stonewort		Rough to the touch. Smell unpleasantly when handled. Spread rapidly.
Egeria densa		White, three-petalled.	For milder areas only.
Elodea canadensis	Canadian pondweed; water thyme; ditchmoss	Insignificant.	Attractive, dark-green foliage.
Fontinalis antipyretica	incombustible water moss		Found in the wild attached to/ growing on submerged stone or wood. Moss-like in appearance.
Hottonia palustris	water violet	Pale purple.	Flowers stand well above water surface.
Lagarosiphon major		Insignificant.	Brittle, narrow, curled leaves thickly clothe plant's branches.
Myriophyllum alternifolium	water milfoil		Excellent hosts for fish eggs.
Nitella gracilis			Thick-growing, thus providing good cover for fry.
Potamogeton spp	pondweed		Can become invasive and choke other plants.
Proserpinaca palustris	mermaid weed		Flowers above water surface.
Ranunculus aquitalis	water crowfoot	White	Will also succeed in stagnant ponds.
Sagittaria sagittifolia	arrowhead	White.	More likely to flower if grown in shallower water.
Utricularia vulgaris	bladderwort	Yellow, snap-dragon-like.	Flowers produced above the water's surface.

The prickly stems of young *Gunnera manicata*.

128

A Selection of Floating Aquatics

Botanic name	Common name	Flowers	Comments
Eichhornia crassipes	floating water hyacinth	Bluish.	Leaf stalks contain cells filled with air, hence their buoyancy. Their long roots are favoured by fish as hatcheries for their eggs. Overwinter indoors.
Hydrocharis morsus-ranae	frogbit	White.	Almost rootless.
Lemna spp	duckweed		Its tiny leaves will eventually form a carpet on the water surface. It is hated by pond-keepers and should never be introduced to large ponds or lakes where it is almost impossible to get rid of.
Stratiotes aloides	water soldier; water aloe	White.	Looks a little bit like the upper section of a pineapple. It rises to the surface when it is about to flower.
Trapa natans	water chestnut	White.	Triangular leaves. Usually treated like an annual in UK climate. Flowers are followed by black, spiny edible seeds, hence common name.

9

CONSTRUCTION AND MAINTENANCE

This section is not laid out to resemble a builder's manual. It is written to point out the pitfalls of pond construction.

FIBREGLASS PONDS

You can build your own pond to your own size but it is a messy and sticky business and, unless you are practised at it, I would suggest you get a contractor to do it for you.

Ready-made fibreglass (or 'semi-rigid') ponds are manufactured in all sorts of shapes and sizes. Their installation is relatively easy so long as you stick to the rules. First, dig a hole which follows the contours of the ready-made pond but which is 15 cm (6 in) wider and deeper. Remove sharp stones and fill in the bottom with sand or turf.

(Turf and other organic materials cannot be used as a cushioner for flexible liners as, once deprived of air, they rot and produce methane gas.) Position the pond, making sure throughout that the edges remain level. This is achieved with a straight piece of timber upon which rests a spirit level.

As you infill the sides so you slowly fill the pond with a hose pipe. Make sure that the infill is well compacted, especially under the shelves for marginal plants, otherwise, the structure can start to buckle under the weight of water.

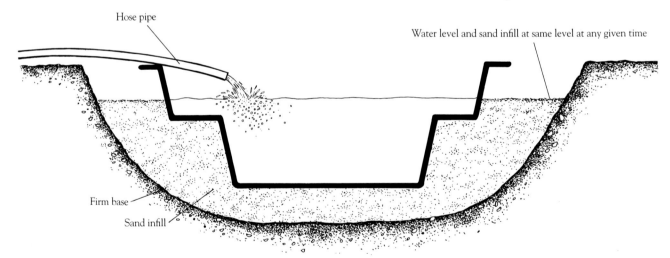

Hose pipe

Water level and sand infill at same level at any given time

Firm base

Sand infill

Fig. 6 Diagram showing the insertion of a glass fibre, semi-rigid, preformed plastic pool container in situ. Note that as the water is introduced into the pool by means of a hose-pipe, the area outside it is filled with sand so that at any given time the water level and sand infill level are the same. This ensures that the semi-rigid container is not put under any undue pressure from the weight of water.

While semi-rigid ponds are comparatively easy to install, one does not wish to be reminded of the fact that they are made of fibreglass. The edges must therefore be cleverly disguised to give the pond a 'natural' look. Rocks, stones and plants all play an important part. The success of the end product depends ultimately upon the eye and artistic prowess of the builder. If the edge is religiously and uniformly followed all the way round with paving stones, it will look truly horrid.

Semi-rigid waterfalls, rivulets, cascades, streams, and other features are also manufactured for those who are more adventurously inclined in the construction of their water gardens.

FLEXIBLE LINERS

Large ponds, lakes (and reservoirs) are nearly always lined with a flexible liner. This is basically waterproof sheeting which should always be laid on a *soft* surface where all jagged materials have first been removed.

Whereas upside-down turves are often used for padding semi-rigid liners (ready-made fibreglass) they, and other organic material, should never be placed directly under a flexible liner because of the resulting methane gas which can quite easily lift the liner up to the water's surface.

Butyl is the strongest (and most expensive) of flexible liners on the market at present. It is manufactured in strips about 1 m (3 ft) wide and these are heat-sealed together if required by the customer.

HOW TO MAKE A CONCRETE-LINED POND

With the advent of the flexible liner (durable polythene sheeting) fashion has gone against concrete-lined pools. Flexible liners are, after all, much quicker and easier to install, and often more reliable. However, concrete-lined pools are efficient retainers of water, so long as a few simple rules are adhered to.

Before you start actually mixing the concrete make sure you have everything to hand, so that the whole job can be finished in one stage, if possible. Here is a list of items you are likely to need:

tarpaulin (to protect the concrete in case it
   starts to rain)
hammer, spade and other tools
water supply
cement
bucket
20 cm (8 in) pegs
chicken wire
galvanized wire (to 'sew' the lengths of
   chicken wire together)

cement trowel
enough sand and chippings.

Dig the hole with the sides sloping at 20° and a sump at the base. The reason for making the sides slope at 20°, is so that the concrete is more likely to stay put once it has been applied, without any need to have to shutter it. Line it with chicken wire and then bang in the pegs 60 cm (2 ft) apart so that they are 15 cm (6 in) proud of the soil surface. These pegs will ensure that you have the vital uniform depth of concrete throughout. Apply the concrete up to the tips of the pegs, and do not forget to remove them before the concrete sets (and infill the holes they leave behind). The concrete should be of a strong mix (one part concrete to three parts all-in aggregate). As soon as it has set (it actually takes 28 hours to set fully) it can be filled with water. This first filling is bound to consist of cloudy water which is caused by the free lime leaching from the fresh concrete. There is no way that either fish or water plants could survive in a freshly made pond such as this until the concrete stops exuding this lime/dangerous-chemical mix.

The pond will have to be emptied and refilled. When the water starts to 'green up' (this indicates that algae is capable of survival in the water) you can safely install its water-loving inmates. It can be several months before the water becomes safe. Often the first fill disappoints, as water escapes over one of the sides before it is properly full. Make sure, therefore, that you get the levels right at the very start, checking with a spirit level.

There are all sorts of proprietary brands of pond sealer available. These are made specifically for concrete. If you want to use a coloured one, avoid blues and greys, as they reduce the reflective properties of the water surface.

HOW TO MAKE A BOG GARDEN

Unless you have a natural boggy area in your garden you will have to build yourself an artificial bog garden if you want to grow successfully the wide range of plants which like these conditions. Many of the plants will grow in drier conditions (see pp.121–4), but tend to be rather disappointing in stature as a result. Many of them are dramatic both in leaf and flower and therefore it is in one's own interest to give them the ideal growing conditions in order to be able to appreciate them in their splendour.

Choose a protected site away from trees' roots. A part of the area can be semi-shaded. Dig out the required area to a depth of about 45 cm (18 in) if you plan to line it with a flexible liner, and around 60 cm (2 ft) if you want to use concrete.

A flexible liner, for example, Butyl would be by far the easiest choice. Stretch a sheet over the site, anchor it down, and then proceed to puncture it just a little. After all, you do want some water to escape, although not too much. Puncture the liner, therefore, with about one hole per 1 sq m (sq yd) over its area.

The bottom of the bog-to-be is first infilled with about 10 cm (4 in) of large stones and rubble. This is covered with approximately the same depth of moisture-retentive organic matter, i.e. turfs, leaves, etc. Bog plants like it quite rich, so fill in the rest with fresh top soil mixed with manure, or whatever else comes to hand.

Lastly, position a hose pipe nearby in case of droughts.

SUBMERSIBLE PUMPS

Submersible pumps prove indispensable for those of us who do not have a natural supply of flowing water in our gardens. They are also cheap to run. Unless you want a very wet garden as a result of a constantly overflowing pond, it is not a good idea to use water from the mains supply.

A submersible pump sits submerged and simply recirculates the same water, either via a fountain, or to the top of a waterfall. In either case the water returns to the pond from whence it came.

They are electrically operated and must, therefore, be professionally installed unless you know exactly what you are doing. If you are having an electrician do it for you, instruct him to attach it to a 'power breaker' in case of accidental damage. Also ask him to position the switch somewhere handy in the house. The idea of water meeting head on with a surge of electricity does not appeal to me. I get visions of old-fashioned bar heaters being dropped into the bath...

Regular maintenance ensures a better and longer performance. It is advisable to remove and

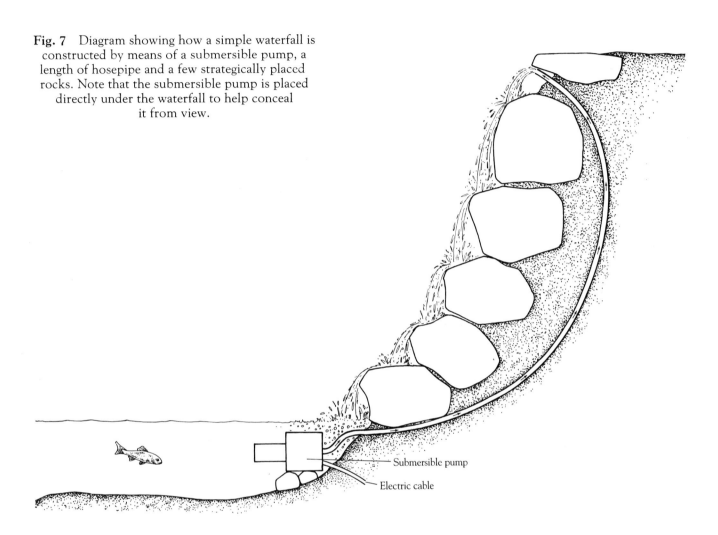

Fig. 7 Diagram showing how a simple waterfall is constructed by means of a submersible pump, a length of hosepipe and a few strategically placed rocks. Note that the submersible pump is placed directly under the waterfall to help conceal it from view.

Submersible pump

Electric cable

service the pump at regular intervals throughout the summer.

Submersible pumps come in different shapes and sizes depending on the amount of water and the height to which they have to recirculate. If you're in any doubt about the power and type of pump you will require, it is advisable to consult your stockist.

WINTER CARE

During the autumn submersible pumps should be taken out of the water and thoroughly cleaned. Make sure the filter is still clean when the pump is repositioned in the spring, having spent the winter in storage.

Smaller ponds can be covered in netting during the autumn to prevent them from being fouled by falling leaves. Larger ponds should be cleaned out with a soft rake. If the leaves are allowed to sit on the bottom of a pond they can turn the water black as they decompose.

Damage by ice to ponds, especially those with rigid liners such as concrete, can be avoided by placing a ball or log of wood on the water's surface. As a result the freezing, expanding water takes its vengeance out on them instead.

Available on the market are electrically-operated immersion heaters, although a section of ice can be thawed out by placing an old-fashioned kettle or saucepan full of boiling water on it. *Never* break ice where there are fish below, as they can be badly stunned or even killed as a result.

PLANTING CONTAINERS FOR AQUATICS

These look like small, square or round perforated plastic waste-paper baskets and they are readily available at most garden centres. They come in various sizes to accommodate different-sized plants. They should first be lined with hessian sacking to reduce clouding of the water with soil particles, etc. The best sort of soil to use in them is a heavy clay medium. It is moisture retentive and helps to reduce water pollution. Well-rotted organic matter can be placed in the bottom of the basket before the clay, as water plants tend to be on the greedy side. Lastly, small stones are placed on the top, like the icing on the cake. These also help to reduce clouding of the water as well as to keep the fish away from interfering with plants' roots.

It is important that aquatic plants are positioned at the correct depth. They may have to be placed on blocks or bricks to achieve this, but make sure you don't damage the liner in the process.

INDEX